Unpacking

Warning
This book contains references to sexual exploitation, abuse and suicide.
If these themes are triggering for you please take care reading this book.

FOREWORD
Acts of Collaboration by Robert Walton   7

MAISIE EVANS
Landing   10
Home as a Person   11
House Mouse   12
Hiding in the Forest   13
Am I Proud of Me Yet   14
Mothering   15
sun   16

Jj
Finding Comfort in Chaos (Part 1)   18
Finding Comfort in Chaos (Part 2)   22
Right Cards to Play   26
It's ten to 3am   29
Leaving the Triangle   30
A Borderline Perspective   31
Going Home for Breakfast   32
Haiku   33
Gaslit   34
The Girl He Took to the Beach   35
Holding Hands with Other People   36
South of My City   38
3 Steps   39
I am   40

DANIELLA WILLEY

If	42
Daniella	43
This is Me	44
Twisted Fairy Tale	46
Letter	48
Depth of Despair	50
Darkest Hour	52
I Don't Want to Die	54
Giving an Education	56
Love I	57
Love II	58
Home Is	60
Cyclone	61
Fairy Tale Princess	62
I Rise	63

FOREWORD

Acts of Collaboration

In his 1757 poem *The Progress of Poesy*, Thomas Gray described poetry as "thoughts that breathe, and words that burn." Over 260 years later, in this stunning collection of poems by Maisie Evans, Jj and Daniella Wiley, we find the truth of Gray's statement: the fire of anger and outrage, fear and anxiety; the flames of questions, criticisms and demands; the heat of hopes, dreams, happiness and humour. These are poems that give voice to the experiences of young women facing up to the challenges and problems of living in this city and the wider world, looking life in the eye and refusing to back down. These are poems of strength, justice, courage that will breathe life and fire into your, and our, understanding of the era we're living through: its chaos, joys and music.

The story of this collaboration goes back a few years, to when Nick Hooper, Chair of the Trustees of Bristol-based charity, *1625: Independent People*, commissioned two brilliant musicians, Harriet Riley and Pete Judge, to compose a jazz suite celebrating the work of *1625*. At the suggestion of jazz entrepreneur Ian Storror, the idea emerged to collaborate with some of *1625*'s young people by asking them to write poems that could be incorporated into the suite as spoken word. I was approached to run some writing workshops, joined by Shagufta Iqbal for a few sessions, aiming for a performance in early 2020. We immediately realised that Danni, Jj and Maisie were poets of immense talent who had been through truly difficult experiences of homelessness but had come through in such a way that, in their words, they refused to be defined by anyone's preconceptions of homelessness. They were themselves, making their individual lives, telling it how it is.

Sadly, Covid locked us down and kept venue doors shut. Undeterred, the poets wanted to continue writing, so our workshops took place on Zoom. And wow! the poems flourished. It soon became clear that far more had been written than could be incorporated into the jazz suite (now called, in one of Jj's phrases, 'Comfort in Chaos'). Not only that: while the poems explored a wide range of experiences, the individual 'voices' of Maisie, Danni and Jj, had emerged with striking persistence. These were voices that had to be heard on their own terms, read, re-read, made permanent in print.

Poetry marriages aren't made in heaven. They happen here on Earth, when people talk, enthuse, take initiatives, act with passion. Through the wonderful support and encouragement of *1625*'s Team Leader for Participation and Volunteering, Chloë Janssen-Lester and publishing expertise of Johanna Darque of Small Press, the book was made.

And so *Unpacking* was packed. Reader, it's a pact of trust that involves you, too, this collection in your hands. You are about to read poems that will provoke, argue, disturb, excite. When Danni asks:

> ' If I told you my thoughts
> And innermost feeling
> Would you really listen?',

she is speaking to you. That word 'really' demands your attention. But if you give it, if you go with the poems as they push at the edges of our expectations. In Jj's words,

> 'standing up for what's right
> with other people',

then you'll experience the profound pleasure of what writing, reading and sharing poetry offers, that unique collaborative experience of what Maisie calls,

> 'Growth
> Confidence
> Connection'.

Reader, connect.

ROBERT WALTON, BRISTOL, 2021.

MAISIE EVANS

Landing

Bare feet on the earth
Body cushioned by old leaf litter
And young saplings
Warm coffee on your (plush) lips
Birdsong dancing
Trees shading me from the
Bright white overcast sky
Little mushrooms
Like fairies
Guarding their ancient treasured homes
Moss thickened tree roots twisting to make a small safe nest

You are not a visitor here
This is where you have been all along
This is your true place
This is where you belong

Home as a person

Warm as my mother's hugs
And wise as her eyes
My home knows me

My home has neatly brushed hair
And an attitude of
I don't care
My home knows me
My room a beating
Pulsing
Womb
Full with manifestation
Of my mind
And my creation

My home never bores me
It keeps me on my toes
And tests me

And then it opens wide arms
Holds my face in its palms
And kisses me
Safely
Goodnight

house mouse

Little brown mouse
I welcome you
To my little brown house
I see you do as you please
feast on my cheese

But why is the elephant so scared of the mouse?
Because it is so tiny?
So incredibly small you are
Your pointed face pierced
With silent glass eyes

Each reflecting a miniature
Warped
Image of myself

I welcome you
What harm can you cause
Dressed to the nines in the finest
Chestnut fur coat
So fine you might even think it was real

Your soft pink nose
Worn as jewellery
Ceramic bubblegum pink
Heart medallion

You turn your nose up at me
And scamper off
Your pea sized belly
Full of cheese

Little brown mouse
I am calling pest control
Your button mushroom babies
Partying
Running rings around my bedroom
Take your cheese and leave
Please

Hiding in the forest

My mind has run away
To hide for a bit
I hope it's okay
When it's safe to come back
I've left a trail of crumbs
On the track
I will find my way
When the light can be seen
A shimmer of hope
Through the unwieldy trees
As I watch them sway
Through the chaos of life
My memories of now
Pass in the brisk night breeze
I can't quite keep up
But I let them go
I will find my way
And soon I will be home

Am I proud of me yet

Now I got myself a job
Done my a-levels with good grades
Through the good and bad days

Am I proud of me yet
Now I pay rent for my own home
And nurture myself
Self nesting
Is the best thing

Am I proud of me yet
For making time for others
For engaging
Giving my time
Giving more than I'm taking

Mothering

Put your feet in your mother's shoes
Feel the weight of time on her heels
Feel the strain on the arches
The pressure to be on the ball
Feel the need to even have feet at all

Look in the mirror at your mum's kind eyes
Wipe her face dry when she cries
Read the wrinkles on her temples from smiling
Through years not knowing
But trying

sun

yoga teacher
wild ginger
wild garlic in her
lunch

her warm routine
the suns salutation

i salute you
you are my sun

Finding comfort in chaos (Part 1)

I struggle to communicate
      I just can't seem to   think straight
this hate   and   debate   in my mind,
I wish I could have a way to   relate
                            to the other part of me
that I don't want you to see
                  because she's not me.

I resent her,
      you won't repent her
            or respect me.
When she makes her
comeback in my bones.
Oh, how she can grow,
                  so strong there
           she can make it home
                                she makes me scared
                                    and not care
                          about anything anymore
and I'm achy and I'm sore
from carrying   this load
for so long,   so I'm sure
that when I'm pushed over the   edge

I doubt I'll even try and move ahead
                and not give in
to see this world like shit.
You're giving me 100
more reasons just to quit.
                      I just don't fit
in with the crowd.
I can be loud.

Just give me a little time,
>> might take a while   to break down my walls.
>> It's hard to be   myself when myself isn't me...

I'll let you see into my bloodstream.
I was still young when it happened;
>> raped,   abandoned,
>> humiliated by someone I thought I trusted,
busted and broken.
No words spoken for nearly a year,
>> embarrassed with my scarring I was careless,
>>> shouldn't have let it happen to me,
>>>> senseless and breathless.
But it wasn't my fault and I'm sure of that now.
It changed how I see the world and the people who let me down.

Years on,
>> frightened and alone
> I tried to help myself,
So I pick up the phone
>> called Crisis
for a way out   of my complicated,
>>> suffocating mindset I had myself in.

I had a part that was happy.
They lost my soul trying to fix me,
> did they not see
> arresting me, tleaving me   alone in a cell
at eighteen,
> no medication for my pain,
>> my suicidal thoughts   choking me
>>> I was stuck in the hell of   my mind.

There wasn't anything holding me down.
From day one I was honest,
and I never wanted to hurt anyone.
    I promise.
    Just myself.
    I can face this
I have to embrace this feeling
because I can't run or hide
from this hatred I have inside

I cannot confide   in someone   I don't know
after the last time   I phoned for help.
    What little faith I have in the system.
        What little faith I have in myself.

It's hard to recognise your face in the mirror
when all I see
is a distorted   reflection of me.
My tired burning eyes;
it's my connection to the other   part of me

Who hates me and   calls me names
says I am to blame for all of these problems I didn't make.
All I did was cry   back then.
Not living with hope.   Numb.
How did I cope?
Losing my passion at such a young age
it threw me off the rails.
I look back at the trail I have made
I'm disappointed   at myself
for letting my mental health
get so bad   again.

Lost faith   in having friends;
                     pushed them away
because the pain
they caused wasn't enough   to forgive.
They didn't need to treat me like shit.
         When my mind was broken
               and my family were ill,
                     but the words that were spoken,
                         I couldn't take him back.
                           Look at him now.
                           I was blinded
                                by trying to not let anyone
down.

These are some of my problems.
My family have tried to be there
         and they've cared.
Caused so many of my issues
but mum you're my guardian angel
         and I'm sorry your baby
             wasn't strong enough to handle
             this clown act of a life.

When I look at myself,
I'm   falling and weak.
The ground shakes beneath my feet
to reveal a girl standing there telling me
if I survived   through this,
this time it should be easy.
And that girl she's me.

Finding comfort in chaos (Part 2)

I struggle with my diagnosis.
But to see a way
to work through this world
I must try and believe in myself.

To get by, survive, thrive
in this complicated life
that I was brought into;
it's almost obvious,
I must be oblivious
to this mysterious, confusing thing
we call society
because the good part of me
has so much to give.

But it's been destroyed
by my experiences
the expectations
my generation
and the ones before us have created.

So congratulations for the manipulations
Dehumanisation
Racism
Xenophobia
Homophobia
Transphobia
Acts of genocide that people have supported
so many added pressures for young people
And they say "our minds are distorted"
and I'm exhausted.

They say we're glued to our phone
"Hungry for attention"
Do I even mention this extension of perfection that we're told to believe?
The unachievable look to aim for
that can lead to anorexia,
bulimia, body dysmorphia
that can lead to unnecessary surgeries,
anorexia, bulimia, body dysmorphia
why can't we restore being happy as a norm?
Respects peoples looks, gender, ethnicity, sexuality
it's about being healthy and happy.

So let's forget about the other people.
The egotistical feeling
that they make us crave for
swipes   likes   retweets
to be seen by everyone on social media.
Because it feeds our
lack of hobbies and interests.
It fuels our disrespect
to survive,
I've learnt life is about acceptance
of whom I am and who you are,
I know it's hard to love yourself
when no one can restore your faith in humanity,
but I can help give you sanity
just take a breath and think it through…
Don't listen to the people who don't believe in you.
Who tell you you're wrong for feeling distressed
depressed, "stop being sad" and "learn to care less"

What's sad is we are silenced.
Forgive us
our invisible illnesses can not be seen,
so we're questioned on our feelings
and on our beliefs?

The way we live our life
because we have been to rock bottom.
We find a way to cope that we are told we will regret in the morning.
But we can't see past the next ten minutes;
let alone tonight.

Well,
bite and criticise me.
Fight my ways and break me,
you can try and see it through my eyes
you'll see it's confusing.
I have days when I am joking
calm easy going
floating on this ocean...

But there's this explosion
provoking my thoughts.
Could set me off any minute
and I'll never win it,
it's an ongoing war
and I'll end up worse than before.

But I don't want you to see me broken.
When I'm choking,
pulling out my hair.
Not that you'd care
because I'm not back in a wheelchair
you can't see the pain I'm in
so you struggle to believe it's there
and you think that's fair?

The Right Cards To Play

For suicide prevention
we need early intervention.
Free talking therapies -
 a place to seek validation
Safe places to be.
To be heard.
      To be seen.
           To be given the opportunity
Of living life with integrity.

Where there's no one doubting your experiences or pain...
Learning how to manage your emotions
You create new coping ways -
so you understand how you feel.

It's hard when life dictates
        so much it can break you.
It takes so much
        till there is nothing left.
I believe in a life that I almost left behind Many times...
I choose now to see the beauty,
Focus on the small.
Give myself the freedom
to not feel anything at all.
      Because "existing"
           Just isn't worth it,

70-75% of people with diagnosable mental illness receive no treatment at all.
(MHFA England)

And living can cause so much pain.
It's hard not to be afraid
of the mistakes that you have made
in a game where you don't have the right cards to play.
When today is difficult,
tomorrow isn't guaranteed.
In no good persons eyes do they believe,
you're not worth the time you need.

You want me to call for help?
 the system is failing, its bailing
You feel that you are falling.
Like they're forgetting us.
Tomorrow will come and I might not be here
So don't question the decisions
don't question the coping mechanisms.
Unless your intentions are to help
create and be
              that early intervention.
Because we're existing in a dimension
where we don't feel
              real at all.

Calling names, projecting shame
Make yourself smaller and listen.
 You might be the reason they don't fall and remission is an option
if you help.

Among the general population **20.6%** of people have had suicidal thoughts at some time, **6.7%** have attempted suicide and **7.3%** have engaged in self-harm.

(MHFA England)

So bring compassion to your conversations.
Be the person that you felt you needed,
be kind, thoughtful and true
one day crisis might come to you.
You'll be left to call a stranger,
breaking down, alone on the phone.
Recalling the moments that led you there.
All the while they know
that the support you need,
Something you're hoping you'll receive
you'll be waiting over 12 months for.
Advocating for yourself feels like a chore
No wonder the young
feel failed by the ones before.

When they don't sort these
problems out at the core.
It's quicker to bring a child into this world than receive the help you need
How fucked up is that?
    So see it for yourself
    Believe in yourself
You yourself can be the intervention
That even a stranger needs.

Call Samaritans: **116 123** | Email Samaritans: **jo@samaritans.org**

It's ten to 3 am.

It's ten to 3 am.
And I'm staring at my wall.
I'm freaking out about sleeping.
I don't think I'll get any tonight.
At all.

The past few nights I've had the same nightmare.
The same face haunting my mind.
The same place where I get lost
and I can't find my way around.
My subconscious is tricking me
so when I scream I can't be found.

I do the same thing each night -
tossing and turning on my bed.
Placing pillows either side of me
none supporting my head.

I feel my face against the mattress
It's a peaceful kind of cold
Not more than I can handle

This insomnia is getting old.
I'm sure tonight will be different.
Being frightened to sleep seems rather immature.
So I'm sure tonight will be different.
I don't want to deal with this anymore.

Leaving the triangle

My hands brushed against the switch.
The lights turn off.
Trying to find my balance
I pulled myself up from the basement,
took off the latch
and opened the panelled door.

I remember the cold burning when the wind hit my face.
My eyes adjust to the busting light.
The silence existed...
But not anymore.
It's now the world behind the door

I breathe in
but not too fast...

I breathe out.

Last night's cold air still lingers.
My chest and fingers feel the breeze.
I start to ease and my body relaxes

A borderline perspective

I logically know that I'm being irrational.
Just my frontal lobe
playing games for my brain again

It's funny -
how my crazy,
can be crazy.
But sometimes
doesn't feel crazy at all.
Just depends if the glass is half full.

Fool.

I paralyse myself with fear.
So I don't end it all
as it's safer to be still
than allow myself to feel,
when the danger in my head
is more than real.

My mind - my emotions.
I was constantly looking for validation
in a world that's only sedation
is cradling your baby.

Maybe, the world needed more time
with less distractions
it only takes a fraction of time
less than a minute
for the trauma to win it.
Win the war
and I've been here before.

So It's safer to be still
than allow myself to feel,
When the danger in my head
is more than real.

Going home for breakfast

Going home for breakfast
Sneaking past the door.
Just when a few hours ago
I was laying on the floor.
It had just turned midnight
The grass tickling my neck
The leaves crunching under my weight.
My back - slowly getting wet.

I watched the moon glow
As it reflected off the dewy ground
No one else in sight
Not one thing,
not even one sound.
And I am found in the depth of nothingness
This vast open green space of nothingness.
But I can not be late for breakfast.
I think to myself.

A place which is restless
Too many noises to see
Metal, concrete streets.

Allergy season
Congested like the M5
Not breathing right now

Condensation glass
My nose against the window
Droplets on my brow

Leaves turning orange
Pumpkin intoxicates nose
Crunch under my feet

Gaslit

        Your
        manipulation fuelled my
isolation, my frustration
          lies with the button for my detonation
 I'm a ticking bomb,
    quickly tick along
          this feeling sticks
      makes your stomach sick
  tick
                tick
        the clocks all wrong
my heightened senses
      makes my body feel like
          I don't belong
              from baby to a lady
      my childhood was fucked
he simply played along.

The girl he took to the beach

She was pre exposed to trauma
  When he told her he loved her.
    Honesty founded the   friendship.
      They spoke about a family - a future
      She's no Saint in the game
     But the way he created a lie
    So big - so unkind.
 That she was losing her mind
The way he reacted
When she woke in a panic
 He ruined her confidence -
   Her self esteem.
     Left her fighting on the edge
      Whilst he was enjoying the
     Holiday by the sea
    Where she was supposed to be.
  After he orchestrated the scene
He came back to see her
 Tell her he forgives her for the dream
   And the only way to be is together.
    He still lied about the girl he took to the
   Beach.
  That was my problem.
Last time it was me.

Holding hands with other people

They say we're broken
because we broke down
their broken system.
Showered in compliments the
police and government
seem to be forgiven.
It's an ideology - it's the policies
that don't sit right with me.

My experience with the police
seemed like a joke when he
dragged me off the floor
put me in cuffs.
All because I didn't want to live in this world.
Enough is enough.

They gear up
march up.
Looking for choke holds.

But holding at the stand
a fragile old man with a plan...
And a sign in his hand
saying the police are none to one
but this bill defies what man
created - freedom of speech,
it's not meant to be police hatred.

They are the face of the government.
The face of the bill.
If it wasn't for George Floyd
and Sarah Everard
you'd be fighting with us still

I know this is hard.
Changing your perspective isn't easy
but the light is shone upon those
with a platform.
Forming and creating safety.

But wide-eyed babies in future generations
will question these things like

Mum,
did you stand on the right side of the plan
holding that man's left hand,
kneeling on the ground
in the middle of a crisis?

Because I don't buy this.

Is it ignorance?

Are people too right-winged to care?
Are people too submissive to the government's stare?

They can't take away the right to protest.
When protesting is the only thing that we have left.

In a society
where over 100,000
people have to sign a petition
to be listened to.
What minority will benefit from this?
Who's gonna listen to you?

So stand with me.
Kneel with me.
Choose to be on
the right side of history.

See, my heart will be there with the people
holding hands with other people
shedding light for other people
getting into fights,
standing up for what's right
with other people.

South of my city

Sitting on an iron bench looking to the south of my city.
Watching the wind take the long grass and branches
dancing
they bend to the breeze.
My hair follows,
blowing in my face and covering my eyes.
Crickets hum and click
my city feels distant.
Why does the world slow down when surrounded by trees?
Why are my concrete streets and red bricks not affected by the breeze?

3 steps

9 am
The house is unusually quiet.
I lean my head out of my bedroom door.
I've hardly been here by myself before.
I sit in the garden,
dressing gown, pants, and hot pink slides
drinking a cup of tea
and smoking my first cigarette -

I will be motivated.

Any trying adult
tries to be productive.

Too long I've procrastinated
about recycling
so my arms filled
plastic bottles,
glass jars
and empty cereal boxes
I struggle unlocking the latch door
with my contorted fingers
trying not to open my
untied dressing gown

3 steps
that's all it took.
3 steps to regret
the lack of clothing
I was wearing
3 steps
1 gush of wind
on the kitchen door
1 slam
and the front door shut.

No keys.
No phone.
Fuck.

I am
After Aja Monet

I am the pebbles where there's meant to be sand,
I am toes instead of fingers on my hands
I am the 5th member of a 4 piece band

I am
the song you hum on the empty bus
I am the drum in your head,
just beating.
Fleeting birds flying away
that feeling when you want someone's touch to stay

I am the rain as you close your eyes to sleep
I am the wind - rustling the trees.
I am an ant you squished on the floor,
I'm a creative young woman
always hoping for more.

I am the child, who grew up too fast,
lasting feelings of loves past.
I am the trauma that he put me through.
I am Cristina, who's lost her shoe.
I am the found shoe, on a pylon in the city tied together by shitty laces.
I sit in self pity for more than 5 minutes
I am the exam you're about to finish.

I am
the moment where you feel at your best
I am the anxiety too big for your chest
I am irrational yet rational alike
I am the excitement
of not going home at night.

I am the green in the decaying leaves
I am the root and flower of all trees
something still growing
still yearning for change
yet I'm still terrified and stuck in my ways.

DANIELLA WILLEY

If

If I wrote from the heart
Would you take it in
If I told you my thoughts
And innermost feelings
Would you really listen?

You're not just working with me
You're taking a part of me
Hearing me for me
The raw unashamed
Unblemished, slightly crazy
Me, Daniella Patricia Louise Willey
You're hearing part of my soul
That no one but me knows

I'm not doing this for money
Or fame I don't want a name
It's the cause that matters
Ending homelessness in Britain
Now I write with my emotion
Feeling I've been crushed, broken,
And emotionally beaten and have
Been walked all over too many times
To remember

So if you really want me to do this
I want the respect I deserve
Because at the end of the day
I know my own self worth

Daniella

Daniella - the name her parents chose to give her.

Daniella has deep brown eyes, you can see into her soul.

Daniella would not hurt a fly. In fact, she chased a spider around her flat for hours, only to try to let it outside to freedom. She's kind-hearted that way, Daniella is.

Daniella: her name means "God is my judge" but she is the judge, jury, executioner of herself. I wish she'd give herself a chance.

Daniella knows her pain does not control her anymore.

Daniella is who she is. She would give her last dime to help others out but often neglects herself. With just a little bit more work she could put one more thing on her already-filled plate but her brain hurts. I wish Daniella knew it's OK to slow down, say no, put herself first.

Hi. By the way, I'm Cassandra, Daniella's best friend. I stop her from going insane, tell her it's enough, she's enough. She is worth more than she takes herself for. I am the best version of her, the person working in the background. Daniella is the little girl who finds it hard to speak, so I speak for her.

This Is Me

Take a moment to relax
Take a breath
In and out
I'll only ask for a couple of minutes
Of your time
Now please
Close your eyes

My story begins at 19
A young woman
Out in the world too soon

Within a year she lost
Her religion her sanity
And almost her life

Her first tattoo says
Never lose faith
But faith lost her
Religion was
The first catalyst
That broke her
Next came the fights
Not only within herself
But with her family
They missed her fall
From grace
The good child
Who never complained

Her parents never
Liked what she did
If only they knew
The men she was with
Replaced the love she desperately craved
The hand that needed holding
The understanding that she's not
Broken but a human being

Then came the day
Her bags were packed up
And a message
Tomorrow you're
Moving into a hostel
The next day she'd gone
Left her childhood home
Homelessness has different
Sides to every story

Now open your eyes
And do you see
That girl in the story
You're staring at her
That girl is a woman
It's me

Twisted Fairy Tale

Once upon a time
That's how stories begin
You usually have heroes and villains
A complicated puzzle that needs to be solved
Then the princess is whisked off by a prince
Happy ending
Resolved ... Tadda!

               B   U   T

My story begins in a hostel
18 years old
Mental health problem
Walking disaster
I had no-where else to go
My first night I could have died
How did I know how to survive?
I'd never lived on my own at 18 years old
I cried myself to sleep
No friends or family
Nobody knew I was homeless
Hidden behind trees and thorns
In a road you would never look down twice

But mental health struggle was the least of my problems
I thought I was pregnant
The man I spent my summer with a monster in my head
I have a twisted relationship with men
He said he was my everything
But he took what he wanted when he wanted it

I just wanted to be loved
To have that fairy tale ending
Pushing myself to be with men who were not right
Who abused me
Used me
Took what they wanted from me
But did not want me

Although I yearned to be with a woman
That was not an option
A black, disabled woman
Who liked women
Living in a hostel
I would have been ridiculed
My family already ashamed of me
So I lived with an abusive older man
At the end of the long winding road
In the hostel that nobody looked at twice

I was not offered therapy
Just a meeting with my support worker once a week
Abused, being used, but unseen
Rape and emotional torture –
He got what he wanted.

This is my twisted fairy tale.

Letter

Dear abuser,

Why are you fixated on I need you
That no other man will do but you

What makes you so special
You need to control what I do
Who I see, what money comes in and goes out of my accounts

I never in my 26 years needed
A knight in shining armour to save me
So why do you believe I need one now

Your twisted reality is scary
I tell you I have issues
That depression has a grip so deep I don't want to live
Next time we argue you bring up my mental health
Like it's a stage 4 cancer
And if I disagree or attempt to leave
It would be the death of me

I see now abuser you are the cancer in me
You make everything about you
It's suffocating
As if life and love were only written about you

But life without you is so much better
Like sticking your head in cold water
And holding your breath
When you leave
The first breath out is such a relief

So abuser I have to say thank you
Thank you for the lessons
Yes, they have hurt oh so much
But I've grown
Thank you for the arguments and fights
Because now I know I'm worth more
Thank you for the hate because
I now love myself more

Dear abuser I hope this letter won't bruise your ego too much
But maybe you need some help
Which I hope in the future you will accept

This comes with love from an abuse survivor

Depth of Despair

I feel the depth of despair coming over me
I feel the burn of the burn-out pulling me
Like a wave
But I'll try not to cave in

Safeguarding young people does not stop
As soon as you shut your front door
The memories of the day come flooding in
Did I do the right thing?
I hope I helped more than I felt I did
My boss is still breathing down my neck
I forgot to hand in the weekly report on time again
You have nightmares when you sleep
Did I lock the door?
Shit! No wait, I'm in my own fucking home
The reporting, reporting, reporting.
I missed breakfast lunch dinner
I haven't left this computer since 8am
It's 11.00 at night
Waiting for a young person to ring, knock
Just send a text saying
They're not coming home but they're OK
They'll come back tomorrow
But you know they won't.

Dealing with young people running away
Police knocking at your door and the 3am
Searches don't get easier
You need to be a mental health warrior
To get through a system
Broken.

Key-working stops working
When we are not on the same page
Moving to the same goal
No wonder young people are running away from home

Darkest Hour

The human condition is ruined
We are so worried about life
We don't live
We walk past people
Without seeing they're there
Did you notice I was homeless
Alone behind the shadows?

No, I did not think so
While you were living
In your happy family together united
I was broken, living a nightmare
Mentally torturing myself
Loneliness broke me but you did not see

Loneliness
Does not creep up
When you've lived with people you trust always being around
Yes, you can say I had people there
But they were not really there
I'm glad I never found myself at the bottom of a bottle
I'm not an addict
Although at times I'm frantic.

My mistake was being lonely
I took someone's kindness for my weakness,
He said I was his queen
I'll treat you right
Yes I'm the queen
With a knight at my side
My knight in shining armour

And here comes the darkest hour
Of my 19 years of life
My nightmare had only just begun
Being homeless is one thing
All the emotions and feelings bubbling
But being stuck with a man 45 years older is more difficult
When I told people they laughed and shuddered
I was the butt of their jokes
45 years older surely you can do better
He's old enough to be your father

No one really asked me why I was with him
Why I put up with the emotional abuse so long
Being raped
Segregated, persecuted
But if they'd asked me, I mean truly heard me for me
They'd see I was a scared girl alone
Who did not have experience of living
Who just knew how to survive, a young girl
Whose every relationship ended being
Emotionally financially desolate
A girl who wanted to be loved so desperately
She would take the abuse because
Loneliness is worse so much worse

My thoughts distorted
Him telling me one thing, my heart saying another
Being with someone's always better than
Being alone in the darkness of homelessness

I Don't Want to Die

We are the forgotten ones
I told the professionals I need help
I continue to tell them I need help
But the doors close on me
I took the pain pills not because
I wanted to die
Nobody wants to die
But it was my last option
I wanted to just to be heard
Taken seriously

Believe me
I don't take my life for granted
But it's a disgrace
Not even the psychiatric people
Will help me
We truly live in a broken system
Where not even doctors will treat us

I'm not ill enough to have a bed in a hospital
I'm not ill enough to be taken seriously
I'm not ill enough to have the psychological help I need

They're gambling with my life
How ill do I have to be to get help

I guess I have to be dead
In my autopsy
The reason given
Intentional
Suicide
Life taken by own hand
Not a proper reason given

Nobody will hear

The countless times I called
111
The crisis line
Samaritans
999

The way I pleaded and begged for help
Had arguments over how unwell I was

I guess feeling dead inside
Is not heart stopping enough
That a suicide note does not mean
I take taking my life seriously

Yes I am in charge of my life
I do understand that
But
Where do you go for help
When no one's there to help
When you
Ask
Ask
and
Ask
And no one's there
What do you do?
Truly
What do you do?

This is not a suicide note
NO
This is my suicide statement
If I die
Let everyone know
I tried

Giving an Education

It's the subtle art of giving a fuck
That matters when you see someone needs help
That you don't just walk by and murmur

What happened to the bubbly girl who had a gorgeous laugh
Those big brown eyes filled with joy
And those laughter lines
Oh yes she's still here

Hostels need to change
We need to make a better future for the next generation
You see the subtle art of giving a fuck that matters

We need education on living
We need education on how to be better
Women men children human beings
The subtle art of giving a fuck

We need to teach young people the skills we need to improve
How to cook how and why we pay bills
And how to maintain your mental wellbeing
Teach young people how to be adults
And make sure our education system does not let them down

Get rid of algebra, the radius of a circle
What I need to learn is how to budget for this week's bills
How to and why I pay tax
The big web of the benefit system

You see knowing about A squared plus + B squared = C squared
Might get me in to Oxford or Cambridge
But will it determine whether I'm eating a home-cooked meal
Or putting electricity on my meter
The subtle art of giving a fuck

Love I

Love it's not easy
Love
Love makes you do stupid things
Love
Love is forgiving
But it never forgets
Love is understood by all animals big and small even by little insects
Love is the giver the taker
Love is the forgiver
Love makes you do crazy things
But to be loved is special
From mother to father
Cousins and best friend
Love is a universal language we all aspire to attain
Love
Love grows and fades
Love helps you to decide to leave or stay
Love is pure
It's simple
Nothing more nothing less
Love will always always be there
That's it
Love is perfect
Nothing more
Nothing less

Love II

Love
A four-letter word we all feel
It does not work that way

Love

Love can make the people
Who you thought cared about you
Pack your clothes and belongings
Into bin liners and suitcase
And tell you you're moving
Into the hostel the next day

Love

Love is being scared of being on your own
Going from being in a house full to the brim with people
To being in a flat on your own
Their words going around in your head like a cyclone

Love

When the clock ticks
Seconds feel like hours
You're doing time
For a crime you never committed
Tick tock tick tock

Love is falling in and out of men's beds
Because if your family don't want you
Maybe the man next to you will
But only for the night

Love

Love I can't trust it
The man I sleep next to
Let alone let myself be loved
Not with him knowing about it

Love only works when
You have first been loved
Love only works when
You let yourself be loved

Home Is

Home is the beating heart of life
Home is keeping the lights on at night
Home is a place of my own
Home is being scared of the police knocking at my door
Home is nice hot baths bubbles all around
Home is being scared of the shouting echoing through walls oh so loud
Home is cars racing by
Home is also being scared to be alone
Being scared to close the door
Being scared of the person I was
Being scared of the person I am
Being scared I'm the only one
Being scared of being scared
Home is what you make of it
Home is precious isn't it

Cyclone

Love is a cyclone
First
This is me
You see the storm
Then it pulls you in
Love is a war of wills
A battlefield
Who will wave
The white flag first
Give in

Do we really know
The people we talk to
Day in day out
Do we trust them
Love is cryptic isn't it
Does not make sense
Is my heart talking or is
My head, do I believe what
They just said

But true love is worth
Fighting for
True love is
If and when you find it.

Fairy Tale Princess

I feel like Cinderella who lost her shoe
I feel like Mulan whose family never understood
I feel like Snow White told to eat the forbidden apple
I feel like Rapunzel locked in a tower
I am Peter Pan in reverse
Scar represents the men I fall for, always wanting power

I feel I'm in High School Musical all singing all dancing
I had the forbidden first kiss but never found my prince
I was Sleeping Beauty whose finger got pricked

I was all the princesses who fell in love young
But I'm waiting for my Prince Charming to come along

I am Elsa always told to let it go
Like Toy Story 3 all of my belongings
Got packed up and put in the attic
Me? I got put in the metaphorical furnace
You call a hostel
And told to survive with little to no hope

My life plays out like a Disney movie
But I'm no damsel in distress
I never needed a prince to save me
I am no princess

I Rise

I am a phoenix
I rise from the ashes
Again and again

You do not know
My story my pain
The things I've gone through
To get me here
Talking to you

I could tell you about
My childhood
My bad taste in men
But then I'd be pitied
Questioned
Put under scrutiny
Maybe not believed
So I distance myself
From my trauma
Tell it from her perspective
The woman I once was

I do understand
There are many sides of a story
Can be told
But I write dark poetry
About sacrifice
Loss of time
Loss of love
Loss of someone
I once was

You see I am not my trauma
I am a phoenix
In the moonlit sky
I rise I rise I rise

Unpacking
First published 2021 by Small Press
Second Edition published Jan 2024 by Jess Haimes & Daniella Willey,
with permission from Small Press

Small Press
Unit 5.16 Paintworks Bristol BS4 3EH
www.tangentbooks.co.uk
*In*disciplinary   smallpresspoetry@gmail.com
University of BRISTOL **poetics**
This chapbook was generously funded in part by the *In*disciplinary Poetics research cluster.

Enormous thanks to Bob Walton for his hard work, generosity and unwavering support of the poets throughout this project. Thanks also to Richard Jones for his wisdom and wonderful publishing know-how.

ISBN: 978-1-914345-11-1

Authors: Maisie Evans, Jj and Daniella Willey.

Illustrations: Maisie Evans

Design and typesetting: Joe Burt

Copyright: Small Press. All rights reserved. The authors have asserted their right under the Copyright Designs and Patents Act of 1988 to be identified as the authors of this work. This book may not be reproduced or transmitted in any form or by any means without the prior written consent of the publisher except by a reviewer who wishes to quote brief passages in connection with a review written in a newspaper or magazine or broadcast on television radio or on the internet.

A CIP record of this book is available at the British Library.

Historic Brisbane
Convict Settlement to River City

REVISED and UPDATED 2004.
PUBLISHED BY PANDANUS PRESS
Second limited edition of 1000 copies.
Pandanus Press, Cutty Sark Studio
10 Matingara Street
Chapel Hill, Brisbane Q. 4069.
Phone: 07-3378-0150
Fax: 07-3378-2744.

DISTRIBUTED BY TOWER BOOKS of Sydney
For trade orders phone: 02 9975-5566
Or fax: 02-9975 5599

Text © Susanna de Vries, 1982, 2003 and 2004.
Design and photography © Jake de Vries.
Photographs © Pandanus Press unless otherwise stated.
The book incorporates material from the 1982
HISTORIC BRISBANE — AND ITS EARLY ARTISTS,
published by Boolarong Publications, Brisbane, 1982.

Apart from any fair dealing for the purposes of private study, research, criticism or review, as permitted under the Copyright Act, this book and its design are the copyright and intellectual property of the persons stated above. They reserve their moral and artistic rights in this property. No part of this book may be reproduced by any process whatsoever without written permission. All inquiries to reproduce text or exclusive pictorial material by any method whatever should be addressed to the publisher.

National Library of Australia
Cataloguing-in-publication
De Vries, Susanna and De Vries, Jake
Historic Brisbane—Convict Settlement to River City
Bibliography and index
ISBN 0-9585408-4-5

1   Historic buildings and structures– Brisbane, Queensland.
2. Paintings, early Australian.
3. Convict days in Brisbane.
4. Brisbane in history.
    994. 3.1

Printed in Singapore by Kyodo Printing Company.

HISTORIC BRISBANE
CONVICT SETTLEMENT TO RIVER CITY

Susanna and Jake de Vries

PANDANUS PRESS

Contents

Foreword	6
Brisbane—A History in Pictures	8
Site plan of Convict Settlement	9
The Moreton Bay Convict Settlement	**10**
The First Stone Buildings	10
The Convict Barracks and the Female Factory	12
Commissariat Store and Officers' Quarters	14
Convicts at Moreton Bay	**17**
Wickham Terrace	**18**
The Windmill and Treadmill	18
Early views of the Convict Settlement	**20**
View from Kangaroo Point	20
View from South Brisbane	21
The First Panorama	23
Plan of Brisbane in 1844	27
The Hospital and Surgeon's Cottage	28
Two Colonial Houses of the 1840s	**30**
Newstead House	30
Bulimba House	31
Three Villages of Old Brisbane Town	**32**
South Brisbane	32
Kangaroo Point Village, 1845	33
Kangaroo Point expands	35
Trained artists visit Brisbane Town	**37**
Conrad Martens	37
Owen Stanley at Moreton Bay	40
The Old and 'New' Customs House	**45**
Pioneering the Fortitude Valley	**46**
Brisbane's First Exhibition, 1876	**47**
Significant Buildings of the 1860s and 1870s	**48**
Parliament House	48
Royal Brisbane Hospital	50
Cintra House	51
The Old Supreme Court	53
The Asylum at Woogaroo	55
General Post Office	56
Wickham Terrace	**58**
Conversion of the Windmill	58
'High Society' on the Terrace	59
North and South Brisbane	**60**

Brisbane Views of the 1860s — 65
View of Brisbane Wharves — 65
Hamilton and Bowen Hills — 65

The Building Boom of the 1880s — 66
Brisbane Boys Grammar School — 66
Brisbane Girls Grammar School — 66
The Queensland Club — 68
The Treasury Building — 70
The Bellevue Hotel — 72
The Former Queensland Museum — 74
The Mansions — 76
Panorama of Brisbane — 1880 — 77
Windermere — 80
Moorlands — 80

The Governor's Residences — 85
Old Government House — 85
The Saga of Fernberg, Bardon — 85

Early days at Milton and Toowong — 87
Mount Coot-tha Road, Toowong — 87
Cook Terrace, Milton — 89
Milton House, Milton — 91
The Regatta Hotel, Toowong — 91
River Road [Coronation Drive] — 92

The Brisbane Floods — 94

The Saga of Brisbane's Bridges — 96
Brisbane's First Wooden Bridge — 96
Collapse of the Wooden Bridge — 98
The First Victoria Bridge — 99
Two more Victoria Bridges — 101
The Indooroopilly Bridge — 103
Seven more bridges — 103

The Brisbane River and its Wharves — 105

Street Scenes of the Past — 108
Boundary Street, Spring Hill — 108
Leichhardt Street, Spring Hill — 110
North Quay — 111

Rowing Clubs and Regattas — 113

A Panoramic View–1888 — 115

South Bank–An enhanced reputation — 118

Queen Street–from Quagmire to Mall — 120

Brisbane's Botanic Gardens — 123
The City Botanic Gardens — 123
Mount Coot-tha Botanic Gardens — 124

Town Halls–Past and Present — 129

Acknowledgements — 130

Bibliography — 131

Index — 133

Foreword

Brisbane evolved from a convict settlement into a state capital and, in area, it became one of the largest cities in the world. The Brisbane City Council administers the largest municipal budget of any council in Australia and is concerned with roads, bridges, parks, water supply, waste disposal, public transport and public libraries.

The riverside city that began life as a convict settlement, divided in two by a meandering river, now has a great variety of amenities. The city is home to the Queensland Conservatorium of Music, Queensland Orchestra, the State Opera and Ballet Companies, the Powerhouse Centre for the Live Arts, a college of art and three universities attracting foreign students. It also has excellent concert halls and theatres, the Queensland State Art Gallery and the Queensland Museum.

The City Council has built the Brisbane Entertainment Centre at Boondall, surrounded by parks and wetlands. Modern Brisbane has all the amenities of a world centre of tourism: an international airport, an international conference and exhibition centre, world-class luxury hotels and award-winning restaurants.

In 1859, when remote Brisbane Town first became a municipality, a successful local builder named John Petrie was appointed its first mayor. In 1930 the title was changed to Lord Mayor.

After John Petrie there have been almost four score mayors and Lord Mayors. However, the names that most residents recall are that of William Jolly, after whom the Grey Street Bridge was renamed, and Clem Jones. Some older residents will remember with gratitude that Clem Jones made his mark by bringing an efficient sewage disposal system to the city, thereby eliminating the need for nightsoil collection by odorous 'honey carts'. Clem Jones also instigated the establishment of the Mount Coot-tha Botanic Gardens, containing one of the most varied and impressive plant collections in the world.

Frank Sleeman is remembered as the Lord Mayor who promoted Brisbane as the venue for the 1982 Commonwealth Games. It was a most successful event, which drew residents together; volunteer helpers contributed their labour and opened the city up as an attractive tourist destination.

Lord Mayor Sallyanne Atkinson's vision for Brisbane as an international city and her flair for public relations helped establish Brisbane as a major venue for international sporting events and conferences.

The hosting of Expo in 1988 marked huge social change as did the fact that outdated regulations banning public open-air eating facilities were lifted. Brisbane, once seen as 'Australia's Cinderella city', became a magnificent subtropical metropolis with open-air cafes, board walks and colourful public gardens. Australians from other states now see Brisbane in a much more positive light than they did in the past. Many foreign visitors have expressed their admiration for the city and its wonderful climate.

The process of change was continued by Jim Soorley. His long period of office as Lord Mayor is identified with the opening up of the Brisbane River by the CityCat ferries, which made travelling by river an attractive option to Brisbane residents and tourists alike. Lord Mayor Jim Soorley also instigated the improvement of run-down areas of the inner city and older waterfront suburbs like Bulimba, which are now linked to the city centre by the comfortable CityCat ferries.

When Jim Soorley retired as Lord Mayor, Tim Quinn succeeded him. Before entering politics Tim Quinn was a history teacher — aptly enough as Lord Mayor he opened the Museum of Brisbane in October 2003. The museum presents changing exhibitions of the city's colourful social history, a subject to which insufficient attention has been paid in the past.

Lord Mayor Quinn also brought the RiverWalk to fruition. RiverWalk was designed to improve river access by providing a 34 km system of riverside pathways and boardwalks, winding its way from Bulimba to Dutton Park on one side of the river and from Breakfast Creek to the University of Queensland on the other side. This initiative is a clear indication that the Brisbane

Plate 9 COMMISSARIAT OFFICERS' QUARTERS. *Formerly known as The Old Parsonage.*
From a set of drawings, Mitchell Library, Sydney.

Plate 10 THE 'NEW' COMMISSARIAT STORE. *Located between William Street and Queens Wharf Road.*
From a set of drawings, Mitchell Library, Sydney.

Plate 11   A recent photograph of THE 'NEW' COMMISSARIAT STORE, Brisbane's second oldest building sited between William Street and Queens Wharf Road. The additional storey was added in 1912–13.

© Pandanus Press.

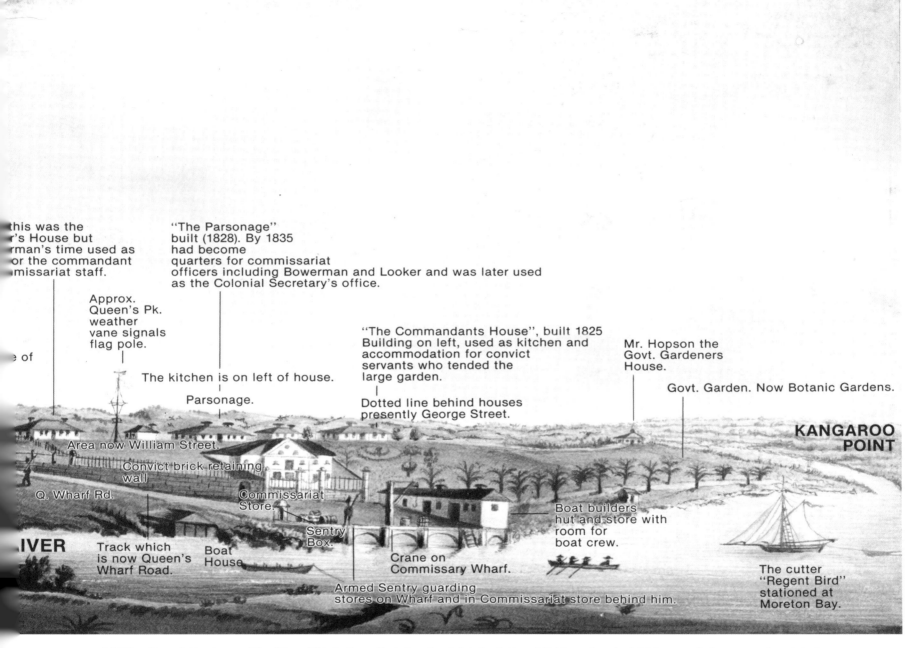

Additional inscription to rear. 21 x 35 cm. This is the earliest signed and dated painting of Brisbane, but the initials can only be seen on the original drawing. Sold Christie's, London to Susanna de Vries and it is now in the John Oxley Library.

The panorama is in tones of grey, known in artistic terms as being painted *en grisaille*. It was painted during the year 1835, when almost 1000 convicts were interned in Brisbane, making it and Sydney the largest penal colonies on mainland Australia.

On the far left Bowerman's painting of the Convict Settlement shows the Windmill with the sails still in place. On the right the artist showed the Government Vegetable Garden [today's City Botanic Gardens] with a bleak and uninhabited Kangaroo Point behind. He expressed the remoteness of the Moreton Bay Convict Settlement and the vast empty landscape stretching away behind it.

Across the river the painting depicts the area presently occupied by the Riverside Expressway. Bowerman shows the Surgeon's Cottage and the Convict Hospital on the left of the junction of today's North Quay and Ann Street. The Commissariat Store is shown in great detail. Goods were unloaded on King William's Wharf [now part of Queens Wharf Road] using the small crane shown in the painting and carried up to the Commissariat Store, where they were checked in by Commissariat Clerks who worked for Henry Boucher Bowerman. Goods were stored in the Commissariat Store until requisitioned by the various departments. Grain was stored on the top floor for export to other settlements. The Commissariat Store is now the headquarters for the Royal Historical Society of Queensland.

The small figure to the left of the convicts, wearing a large sun hat, would have been the convict overseer. The overseers were chosen not for good behaviour but because they were brutal men who could be relied on to terrorise the other convicts and maintain strict discipline. The convict overseers' sentences were shortened by one year for every two years they performed the job. Overseers could request the flogging of members of the chain gang if they misbehaved or did not work hard enough.

Overseers were quartered in their own separate huts rather than in the main Convict Barracks, since they were so hated they risked being murdered in their sleep by other convicts.

Bowerman's detailed panorama and the earlier pencil sketch show fences which ran along the edge of today's Elizabeth Street and separated the homes of the Officers, the Commissariat Staff and the Commandant from the rest of the Settlement. The fences may have been erected to prevent pilfering by the convicts. They started at the Lieutenant's Quarters, ran past the Commissariat Quarters and down to the Commissariat Store on today's William Street. The fences would have provided some protection to the Officers and a deterrent to convicts who might have contemplated breaking into the Commissariat Store, where the Settlement's supplies of tools and dry foodstuffs were kept.

The neat fences and small brick cottages give an incongruous air of respectability to the Convict Settlement with its grim reputation and high death rate from tropical diseases and the effects of severe floggings.

In the panorama Henry Boucher Bowerman has drawn one of the very few carts allowed into the Settlement. The artist has also recorded many other interesting details, such as the alarm bell on a tall pole to the right of the Prisoners' Barracks. The purpose of the bell was to awake the convicts at daybreak.

One of the most fascinating features in this panorama is the fact that the artist shows convicts working in an area that later became known as Queens Wharf Road. Depiction of convicts at work enhances the historic value of this unique watercolour, because this phenomenon is rarely shown in other Australian art of the time.

We see convicts dragging handcarts loaded with supplies or building materials. Horses and oxen were not used in the settlement, but some bullocks were available to move the heavier loads.

The cutter *Regent Bird*, shown in the pencil sketch on plate 16, is also depicted in Bowerman's panorama. The cutter was used by the Army, the Convict Department and the Commissariat Department to transport supplies to the stores at Dunwich and the pilot station at Amity Point and upriver to Ipswich. It was crewed by seamen, who lived in a boathouse near the wharf, rather than by convicts, who could have mutinied and escaped in it.

River, arguably the city's most important natural asset, becomes more and more appreciated by the City Fathers and Brisbane's citizens alike.

In March 2004 Brisbane voters elected Campbell Newman as their new Lord Mayor. There was no precedent in Brisbane's history for having a Lord Mayor from one political party while the majority of the Councillors are from an opposing party.

Lord Mayor Newman is committed to improve Brisbane's road system, which has become increasingly congested during the past twenty years. Being a civil engineer by profession, he has an excellent insight into the way his aim can be achieved most effectively.

Campbell Newman is dedicated to enhance the traffic flow by building additional tunnels and bridges, by augmenting arterial roads and by improving and extending the public transport system. The first step in that direction will be the construction of the 'Green Bridge', which aims to provide a pedestrian, bicycle and bus connection between Queensland University and the eastern suburbs.

In July 2004, Lord Mayor Newman presided over celebrations to mark the start of work on Brisbane's important cruise ship terminal, which will bring many thousands of affluent tourists from all over the world to this unique River City.

Brisbane–A History in Pictures

This book portrays the development of Brisbane as seen in some of its first paintings, drawings, maps and photographs. Many of these historic documents reveal the bleakness and isolation of the convict settlement.

Very few cities in the world have their first days recorded. Luckily, a few images of Brisbane's convict past have been recorded in drawings by Henry Boucher Bowerman and William Looker.

The Moreton Bay Settlement was later replaced by a primitive frontier town, inhabited by men without wives, men who drank themselves often insensible.

Unlike Old Sydney Town, the Moreton Bay Settlement had no artists among its twice-convicted thieves and murderers. The area's first artist to sign his work was Commissariat Officer Henry Boucher Bowerman. He was followed in the first days of free settlement by squatter-artist George Fairholme. As a boy of 18 Fairholme helped his childhood friends, the Leslie brothers, explore and open up the Darling Downs for settlement.

In 1847 the maritime artist Owen Stanley visited Brisbane and made at least two watercolours of the Town. Conrad Martens, Australia's finest classical landscape artist, visited Brisbane in November 1851 to obtain commissions from Brisbane's wealthier residents. Martens' view of the Brisbane River commissioned from the artist by Lord Henry Montagu-Douglas-Scott has been chosen for the jacket of this book.

Martens was the first professional artist to visit Brisbane and three of his pupils also drew Brisbane. The first was an intrepid pioneer of the Darling Downs, Lady Eliza Hodgson [Dowling], who was Queensland's first woman artist. Lord Henry Scott, son of a Duke, who visited early Brisbane Town on his 1853 world tour, painted views here as did wealthy traveller Henry Grant Lloyd, escaping from the cold of his native Tasmania.

These artists recorded the amazing land and building boom of the 1880s, when some of Brisbane's most imposing stone buildings were built.

Plate 1 shows what is believed to be the first private cottage in the settlement. It was the home of Captain Coley, a former sea captain who, after separation from New South Wales, was appointed Sergeant-at-Arms in the new Legislative Assembly.

Plate 1. ALLEGEDLY THE FIRST PRIVATE HOME IN BRISBANE. *Wood engraving from* **The Picturesque Atlas of Australasia, 1888.** *Private collection.*

Plate 2. ANDREW PETRIE'S HOUSE *with its shingled roof stood on the corner of what is today Queen and Wharf Streets. Redrawn from a photograph.* © *Pandanus Press.*

Site Plan of Convict Settlement

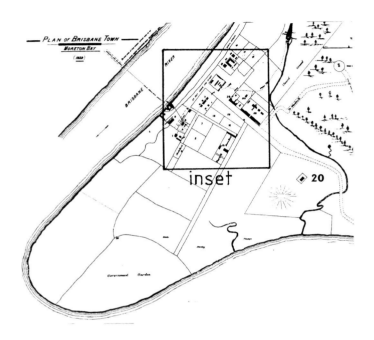

Plate 3. LOCATION PLAN OF BRISBANE'S EARLIEST STRUCTURES. Information obtained from Plan of Brisbane Town to Accompany Major Barney's Report of May 1839.

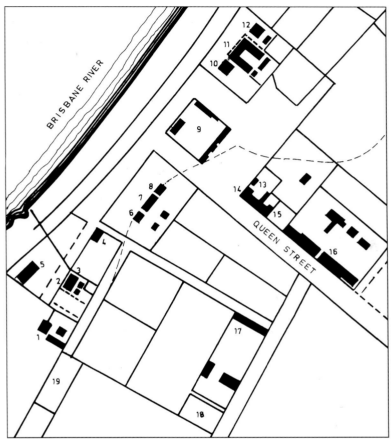

Legend

1. Commandant's Quarters
2. Commissariat Officers' Quarters
3. Chaplain's Quarters
4. Police and Commissariat Offices
5. Commissariat Store
6. Officers' Quarters
7. Military Barracks
8. Guard Houses
9. Lumber Yard
10. Military Hospital
11. Convicts' Hospital
12. Surgeon's Quarters
13. Solitary Cells
14. Superintendent of Convicts
15. Soldiers' Quarters
16. Convicts Barracks
17. Barns
18. Piggery
19. Stock Yard
20. Female Factory [see map to the left]

The Moreton Bay Convict Settlement

Originally, Redcliffe had been chosen as the site for a convict settlement, but the area proved to be fever-prone and difficult to defend. So in May 1825 Commandant Henry Miller decided to move his troops and the convicts they guarded from swampy Redcliffe, where swarms of malarial mosquitoes bred. Miller had already experienced some of his men dying of malaria when serving with Wellington's army in Spain.

At Redcliffe he had also been worried that the Aborigines might attack the settlement in force. They had already raided the fledgling settlement's stores in search of sugar and flour, which they loved.

Captain Miller had selected the triangle of land bounded on two sides by the Brisbane River, which he hoped was a safer area. Today this area is Brisbane's central business district and is fringed by the perennially busy Riverside Expressway, the tall towers of Eagle Street and the tranquil City Botanic Gardens.

The Captain justified moving tents, stores, soldiers, their families and the convicts they were guarding by claiming that the new site had better water and would be a far easier area to defend against Aborigines who, not unnaturally, resented the presence of white men.

The Ngundari, Jagura [pronounced as Yagura] and some other Aboriginal family groups lived by the river and roamed through the area. These Aboriginal groups had a well-defined code of kinship laws, initiation ceremonies and legends.

The Aborigines were removed from the North Brisbane area when it became a convict settlement, but they continued to inhabit the South Brisbane area.

The First Stone Buildings

During the harsh regime of Captain Patrick Logan, the first stone buildings of the Moreton Bay Convict Settlement were erected by convict labour. A series of small but historically important pencil sketches of these first buildings, titled *Moreton Bay Settlement, New South Wales, 1832*, are held in the collection of the Mitchell Library, Sydney; several are reproduced here.

The sketch of the Convict Barracks is signed with the name W.C. Looker in small letters on the edge of the perimeter wall. His name appears in records held by the John Oxley Library of civilians and Army personnel serving at Moreton Bay. Commissariat Officer William Looker [1793–1872] entered the Commissariat Service as a clerk attached to the Treasury in London, worked as a Senior Audit Clerk in Canada and was commissioned Deputy Assistant Commissary-General on 15 July 1826.

Looker served at Moreton Bay from November 1830 till January 1835 and drew the sketches of the main buildings at the settlement during that period. He left Moreton Bay for Hobart with his family aboard the ship *Guardian* on 22 January 1835. He returned to London in 1849 and died there in 1872.

William Looker and Henry Boucher Bowerman were the first visual recorders of what would become Brisbane. Looker's drawings were made to accompany an official report sent to London to show the Colonial Office how the Convict Settlement was developing.

Looker's drawings and Boucher Bowerman's panorama [plate 17] are the only extant views of the Georgian style buildings of Moreton Bay which, with the exception of the Commissariat Store [still standing on William Street], were demolished to make way for Victorian buildings in what became Brisbane Town.

The Military Barracks were built in 1828, designed to accommodate the 100 soldiers who garrisoned the Convict Settlement.

Today's Queen Street developed along the line of the first convict buildings. Care was taken to place the buildings above the Brisbane River's flood line.

A large fenced area in front of the Convict Barracks was called the 'Lumber Yard'. Looker's drawing shows a fenced yard behind the railings, which contained storerooms and workshops for convict blacksmiths, carpenters, wheelwrights, tailors and shoemakers.

Plate 4. THE LUMBER YARD. This was the first Military Barracks Compound.

From a set of drawings, Mitchell Library, Sydney.

Plate 5. THE NEW MILITARY BARRACKS AND SUBALTERNS' QUARTERS
Built on the site of the Treasury Building, corner Queen and George Street and facing William Street.

From a set of drawings, Mitchell Library, Sydney.

Plate 6   THE COMMANDANT'S RESIDENCE.
From a set of drawings, Mitchell Library, Sydney.

In this work area convicts made their own uniforms, leather caps and boots as well as soap and candles for the whole settlement. They also made nails and iron bolts which were used on rough pieces of furniture made from local timber for the Officers' Quarters and Soldiers' Barracks.

Captain Patrick Logan arrived in 1826. He enlarged the Convict Barracks and built a gaol and the Convict Hospital. In 1831, the settlement needed more guards, so larger Military Barracks were built. At that time Captain Clunie was Commandant of the settlement.

Captain Clunie was followed by Captain Fyans in 1835, Major Cotton in 1837, and by Lieutenant Gravatt and Lieutenant Gorman in 1839. Cotton and Gravatt are commemorated in the names of Mount Cotton and Mount Gravatt. After the Convict Settlement closed and Brisbane was opened up for free settlement as part of New South Wales, the stone Military Barracks were used as the Registrar-General's Office.

The Commandant's Residence was a prefabricated wooden cottage, constructed in Sydney and sent by ship to be erected at Redcliffe and later moved to William Street. The cottage had brick chimneys and a free-standing brick kitchen to reduce the risk of fire, which was a constant hazard in these timber buildings.

The Convict Barracks and the Female Factory

The Convict or Prisoners' Barracks were built from 1827 to 1830 to house up to 1000 convicts. Built of stone, it was the largest building in the settlement. Its location determined the future layout of Queen Street. It was used from 1860 to 1868 as a Court House and home for the first Queensland Parliament.

Plate 8 depicts the infamous Female Factory, built in 1829 on the site of today's General Post Office in Queen Street. Letters from Commandant Clunie and Colonial Secretary Alexander Macleay refer to the urgent necessity of enclosing the Female Factory behind a high wall. This was to protect the women from harassment by the sexually deprived male convicts and their guards.

Prior to the construction of the wall the lack of security at the Female Factory, ironically known as a reformatory, was highlighted by the fact that Captain Richards of the ship *Governor Phillip* and clerk William Holden, accompanied by two drunken officers, broke in one late night after a party. A bottle of rum secured the sexual favours of the women for the night.

Plate 7   THE CONVICT OR PRISONERS' BARRACKS

From a set of drawings, Mitchell Library, Sydney.

Plate 8   THE FEMALE FACTORY. Now the site of the G.P.O. in Queen Street.

From a set of drawings, Mitchell Library, Sydney.

The men were spotted in 'compromising positions' by the guard. Dr Cowper was also involved. The Commandant, who felt that the doctor should have known better, dismissed him.

It seems incredible that as many as 138 women convicts lived and worked under hot, insanitary and cramped conditions in this small building with an outside kitchen and one lavatory. The women were employed to pick oakum from frayed ropes for use in caulking the settlement's boats. They also made ropes and rough convict clothing from cloth woven by convicts at the Parramatta Female Factory.

The Female Factory was simply a workplace for these unfortunate women whose lives were often worse than those of the male convicts. It was unlikely that any of the women would ever earn enough to return to their homes. For many female convicts, prostitution was the only escape once they had completed their sentence.

The Female Factory later became a gaol and still later a police court. In the early days the compound yard on 'Gaol Hill' was the scene of the annual distribution of red woollen blankets to Aborigines who lived in the area.

In 1871 the new Brisbane GPO was built on the site of the Female Factory. Gaol Hill had to be levelled for construction of the GPO.

Commissariat Officers' Quarters/Commissariat Store

The Commissariat Officers' Quarters, built in 1828, was formerly known as the Old Parsonage. It housed Chaplain Vincent, his large family and servants. Worship services for officers and other free persons were held in the hall of the house.

In 1830 the building was divided into two apartments, which were occupied by Commissariat officers and surgeons. On plate 9 a second entrance door is visible at the extreme left of the verandah, which was added just before that drawing was made.

The Moreton Bay Settlement required a great deal of equipment, which had to be stored in the convict-built Commissariat Store where Henry Boucher Bowerman may have had his office. Goods and equipment were also stored in the Lumber Yard. The first Commissariat Store was a barn located next to Mr Parker's hut near the corner of Elizabeth and Albert Streets. Parker was the settlement's Superintendent of Agriculture.

The barn-like structure was built in wood soon after the establishment of the settlement. But the old store was soon not large enough to fulfil the settlement's requirements, so the new Commissariat Store was built some time between 1827 and 1829. The old store was retained as a barn and slaughterhouse.

The new Commissariat Store was erected between William Street and Queens Wharf Road, being handy to the wharves and the river. It was built of dressed stone with two feet [600 mm] thick walls to prevent forced entry. Tools, seeds, grain and various other provisions were stored inside the building.

The small iron-barred door, still in place today, made the Commissariat Store defensible. Wooden doors on the western entrance were originally sheathed with iron to enable them to resist an onslaught. Grey ironbark was used for the floor bearers and rafters. The backbreaking work to cut and form the timber members was carried out by convicts. The floor bearers have remained sound and straight throughout the years. Handmade nails were used to fix the floorboards of grey gum and tallow wood, which were pit-sawn and tongue-and-grooved with hand tools.

The foundations and walls have a base course and corner stones of Brisbane tuff, and walls up to the new portion are built of freestone. Although these walls have been submerged by successive floods they show little sign of weathering. The inscription on the front of the building reads '1829' and is still clearly visible today.

In 1912–13 an additional storey was added and the original roof was replaced.

The Commissariat Store has now been restored and houses the Thomas Welsby Library and the Royal Historical Society of Queensland's headquarters. It also houses the Penal Settlement Museum.

Convicts at Moreton Bay

Only hardened criminals, known as 'old lags', and prisoners re-convicted of further crimes were sent to Moreton Bay, which acquired an evil reputation for violence and a high death rate from imported tropical diseases.

Convict numbers peaked at 947 in 1831 but dropped to 374 in 1835 as the settlement was closing. The remaining convicts were sent back to Sydney.

Most convicts wore a leather hat, made by leatherworkers in the Old Lumber Yard, and a rough grey jacket, which had to be painted with the word 'Felon'. The convicts sentenced to wear leg irons were given trousers buttoned at the side, so that at night they could be unbuttoned and removed over the leg irons.

Leg irons were made up and fitted by a convict blacksmith. A cuff made of leather was fitted to each ankle to prevent sores. A length of chain was welded between the two irons with a string attached so that it would not drag along the ground. One of the convicts in Augustus Earle's picture is holding up this string with his left hand. The heaviest chains weighed about 18 pounds [eight kilos], and encircled each ankle over the leather cuff.

The visiting Quaker missionary James Backhouse kept a diary of his visit to Moreton Bay in 1836, describing the settlement as a place 'where some of the most vicious portion of the population of Great Britain and Ireland was placed'. Robbery, murder and homosexual assaults were rife amongst a population of desperate men. Many of them were convinced they would die at Moreton Bay of disease, overwork or severe floggings. Convict labourers worked in chain gangs of 15 men.

The missionary James Backhouse recorded in 1836:

> All male prisoners arriving at Moreton Bay are continued in irons for nine months, at the expiration of which the irons are removed, unless misconduct has occurred or the parties have been sentenced to wear irons during the term of their transportation to the settlement. In the latter case they continue in irons during the whole period of their sentence.

Plate 12   CONVICTS IN THE COLONY OF NEW SOUTH WALES. *Detail from a pencil drawing by* AUGUSTUS EARLE *[1793–1838], later published as a lithograph in* **Views of New South Wales.** *London 1830. It is one of the few illustrations showing convicts.*

Authors' collection.

Wickham Terrace

The Windmill and Treadmill

Historically, the Windmill is Brisbane's most important and unique structure. According to various historians it was built in 1828 so that the Moreton Bay Settlement might grind its own maize and corn for its food supply.

By 1829, the storekeeper informed the Deputy Assistant Commissary-General that the Windmill needed continual repairs and would not operate in calm weather.

The constant malfunction of the Windmill made the construction of a treadmill, to be operated by convicts, desirable. Without regular supplies of maize flour the settlement would have had periods when insufficient food was available, because supplies coming by ship from Sydney often took over a month to arrive.

In 1837 Scots-born Andrew Petrie [1798–1872] arrived in Brisbane. He was appointed Superintendent of Works in the settlement and later became Brisbane's first and most important building contractor. Petrie managed to repair the Windmill and, with enough wind power, it continued to operate under sail until 1841.

However, utilising the Treadmill for grinding maize during calm weather was only a secondary consideration, as it was primarily used as a means of punishment, other than flogging or solitary confinement.

Punishment for relatively minor offences or failure to complete the necessary work quota could mean the convict received a flogging of 25 lashes or a 14-hour stretch on the Treadmill, with a short rest period when four convicts were allowed off the treads at a time. The work was extremely hard in the hot weather; men worn out with exhaustion were known to fall from the treads.

Quaker missionary James Backhouse recorded in his diary that the Convict Treadmill was

> generally worked by twenty-five prisoners at a time but when used for special punishment, sixteen are kept upon it for fourteen hours at one time.

Undoubtedly, long hours of this tiring work in a sub-tropical climate by prisoners already undernourished by a poor diet, while wearing eight kilo leg irons, would have contributed towards the relatively high convict death-rate of the Settlement. 'A day on the Treadmill replaced the lash for less serious offences. Men on the Treadmill endured an existence which robbed even death of its terrors', wrote one convict with feeling.

An official Report of Convict Deaths, made in September 1829, states that a prisoner named Michael Collins became 'entangled in the machinery of the tread wheel and was killed'. Memoirs of various convicts at the Settlement describe cases of men dying of exhaustion after long hours on the Treadmill.

William Ross, a prisoner at Moreton Bay from 1826 to 1833, later published an account of the life of a convict at Moreton Bay in his book *The Fell Tyrant*. In his book he complained how

> the brutality used on this piece of machinery is beyond the power of a human being to describe. The unfortunate men are continually falling from it apparently in a lifeless state.

Several other sources of information indicate that Ross's allegations were greatly exaggerated.

Nevertheless, high rates of hospital admission for the summer of 1829 were recorded from heat exhaustion after arduous work on the Treadmill.

The convicts had to grasp an overhead rail with both hands and tread the 9-inch [230 mm] wide steps as if walking continuously upstairs. They had to step out briskly or be bruised on the shins by the next tread as it came round. In the steamy heat of summer the convicts were forced to tread unremittingly, as though on a long march. It is obvious that those with the heavier irons had the hardest job to keep up.

Andrew Petrie described hearing the click, click of the convicts' irons as they kept in step with the wheel.

Directly after the Moreton Bay Convict Settlement was closed and the free settlers of Brisbane Town started to arrive, the Treadmill was dismantled.

Plate 13 [above].
THE TREADMILL, adapted from a drawing by the late Geoffrey Ingelton.

Plate 14 [left].
THE WINDMILL AS IT WOULD HAVE LOOKED BEFORE THE SAILS WERE REMOVED.
An artist's impression, drawn by Jake de Vries.

© *Pandanus Press.*

Early Views of the Convict Settlement

View from Kangaroo Point

The unsigned but historically important sketch of Moreton Bay Settlement, depicted on plate 15, is a view from Kangaroo Point. It shows the location around today's Queen Street after further development had taken place [see also inset map on page 9].

Visible on the left side of the sketch are maize plants and banana trees growing in the Government Gardens [today's City Botanic Gardens]. Near a small hut or corn crib convicts stripped maize kernels from the cobs before loading the maize into sacks and carrying it to be ground by the Windmill, which in the picture still has its sails.

The low wall of a piggery to the left of the corn crib confirms that pork was available.

Sited at some distance from the all-male Convict Barracks was the Female Factory. Near the building was Wheat Creek, which ran from today's Roma Street, across

Plate 15. *MORETON BAY SETTLEMENT, NEW SOUTH WALES, FROM KANGAROO POINT. Attributed to HENRY BOUCHER BOWERMAN. Pencil drawing, undated but c. 1833–35. It gives the rear elevation of the buildings shown in Bowerman's panorama from South Brisbane [plate 17].*

Rex Nan Kivell Collection, National Library, Canberra [NK 211].

Adelaide Street and along Creek Street and passed through a low-lying swamp area. The picture shows a plank bridge built across a small creek, called Frog's Hollow, which is where Margaret Street is today.

Near the centre of the picture, secure inside a fenced stockade, are the Military Officers' Quarters, including the Subalterns' Quarters with their separate brick kitchens.

On the site of today's Queens Park is a tall flagstaff, which was used to hoist flags as a signal to incoming shipping. To the left is the Commandant's house.

Convicts in the chain gang are breaking harsh stony ground with picks and shovels. It is impossible to pick out details but from other sources we know they wore uniform trousers, jackets and leg irons and chains.

Guarded by a convict overseer and an armed soldier, the convicts struggle away to fulfil the day's work quota. Nearby is a pair of what are probably young subalterns standing on the bank of the river. Only one solitary hoop pine remains after the bush had been cleared by the chain gangs. Andrew Petrie claimed that the tree had been left standing so convicts could be tied to it and flogged by Gilligan 'the flogger' for whatever breaches of discipline they had committed.

Convict William Ross's partly fictitious book *The Fell Tyrant* has recently been republished with annotations by Dr John Steele and Dr Jennifer Harrison. In his book Ross described how

> the tyrannical overseers urged men to work beyond their strength while exposed to the boiling sun, often in a state of nudity, exhausted with fatigue and starvation, wearing irons of 18–20 pounds on their legs.

The irony is that William Ross himself was an overseer and was, in fact, among those he pretended to hate.

The *Official Regulations for Penal Settlements,* issued by Governor Darling in 1829, describe how plough horses and oxen were banned and replaced by convict labour. However bullocks were used to transport the heavier loads. The *Official Regulations* stated:

> As an aversion to honest Industry and Labour has been the Chief Cause of most of the Convicts incurring the penalties of the Law, they shall be employed at some species of Labour which they cannot evade. The Convicts are to be employed exclusively in Agricultural operations, when Public Buildings or other Works of the Settlement do not absolutely require their Labour. It has consequently been directed that the Spade and Hoe shall be substituted for the Plough, which will greatly diminish the demand for Horses and Oxen, and be the means of keeping the Convicts constantly and usefully employed. Convicts under Colonial Sentence shall be steadily and constantly employed at Hard Labour from Sunrise till Sunset, One Hour being allowed for Breakfast and One Hour for Dinner during the Winter Six Months; but Two Hours will be allotted for Dinner during the Summer.

The memoirs of William Ross record that 'six out of ten prisoners would rather be hanged than drag out a life of such misery'. Some are supposed to have killed another convict or an overseer to be hanged.

By 1829, Moreton Bay was the largest penal settlement on the Australian mainland, with over 1000 convicts. Governor Bourke reduced that number to 300 by 1837 and was also responsible for establishing the Female Factory for re-convicted women.

View from South Brisbane

The scene depicted on plate 16 seems to be a preliminary sketch made by Commissariat Clerk William Looker or by Henry Boucher Bowerman himself for his larger and more detailed panorama [plate 17]. It tells the viewer a great deal about daily life in the Convict Settlement, where convicts were working along what is now North Quay and Queens Wharf Road.

On the left of the sketch is the Children's Graveyard, used to bury the children of the soldiers. Due to poor hygiene and diseases brought in from the tropics the death rate among the children was exceptionally high.

A tank [near today's Tank Street] served as a water reservoir for the settlement. However, for a period of time water in the tank was polluted, which would have contributed to the high infant deaths. On medical advice steps were later taken to remedy the pollution problem.

The pencil sketch shows convicts working in sawpits, sited where today's Herschel Street joins the Riverside Expressway. The cedar and hoop-pine logging gangs from South Brisbane floated tree trunks across the water and some logs are lying at the river's edge, while others have been stacked upright to dry. The Brick Kiln, to the left of the sawpits, was started in 1826. It was used to fire bricks for various buildings in the settlement.

South Brisbane was still the preserve of Aborigines but two decades later the area rivalled North Brisbane as a centre for warehouses and wharf space.

From this sketch and from the map, shown on page 9, it is possible to trace the evolution of Brisbane's first streets: North Quay, William Street and Queen Street developed from the location of the buildings and from tracks made by the convicts and their guards between them and the maize and vegetable plantations. When Brisbane opened for free settlement these plantations became grazing land for cows and later were turned into the Botanic Gardens.

The central area of the drawing relates to Henry Boucher Bowerman's panorama [plate 17] and Captain Barney's map. The drawing on plate 16 and Bowerman's panorama have altered the orientation of the Convict Barracks, so that the more imposing western elevation faces the viewer. This indicates that these pictures were intended to create a favourable impression of the work performed by the Commissariat Department.

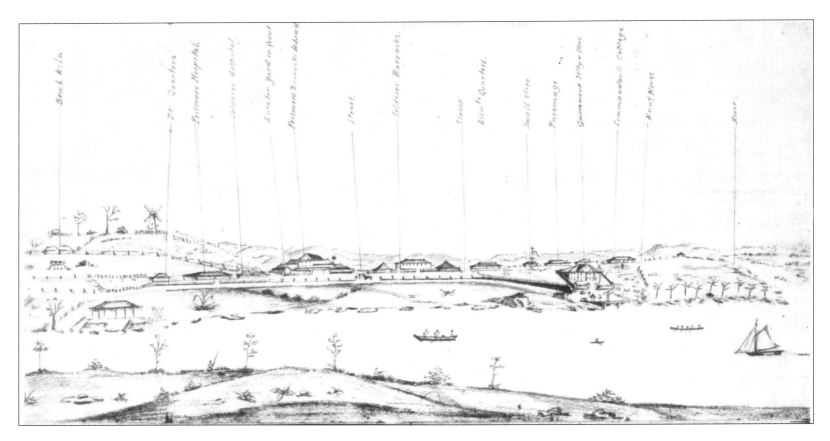

Plate 16. THE MORETON BAY SETTLEMENT DRAWN FROM SOUTH BRISBANE, c. 1835. Pencil sketch, unsigned, but believed to be a preliminary sketch, possibly by Henry Boucher Bowerman or William Looker, with the key to the buildings added by another hand.
Mitchell Library, Sydney.

On the extreme right are the flower beds of the Commandant's Garden which were tended by a sadistic convict named Gilligan, who also flogged the convicts as part of his official duties.

The Moreton Bay drawings are unusual in showing convicts at work. The majority of convict or 'free' artists working in Australia preferred to forget the grim realities of the convict system, which they believed lacked artistic appeal. In Sydney, convicted artist-forgers like Joseph Lycett and Thomas Watling concentrated on the latest buildings in the colony and unfamiliar flora and fauna.

The pencil sketch highlights the importance of the Brisbane River to the Convict Settlement, where, due to the lack of paved roads, the river acted as a highway for the transport of men and goods. Bowerman's watercolour shows the cutter *Regent Bird* to the right. This cutter was an important means of transport for the Settlement.

The First Panorama

Henry Boucher Bowerman's *View of the Convict Settlement* from the site of today's South Bank Cultural Centre is one of Brisbane's earliest visual records [plate 17]. This, the first signed painting of the Convict Settlement, is a key picture for a study of Brisbane's history.

The painting is mentioned by the editor of the *Brisbane Courier* in November 1862, who was shown it by Cordelia Bowerman, daughter-in-law of the painting's artist Henry Boucher Bowerman. She showed it to the editor who told her that no one in Brisbane wanted to see or buy a painting of the convict era.

In the *Brisbane Courier* of November 1862 the editor described the watercolour as 'an interesting memento of the old times but one that free settlers in Brisbane would prefer to forget'. His comments are interesting and show how people wanted to obliterate memories of the convict era in the days of Queen Victoria.

Cordelia Bowerman was involved in a considerable scandal and was about to return to England with her children as her husband, son of the ultra-respectable Henry Boucher Bowerman, had been jailed for assaulting the Colonial Secretary, Sir Arthur Manning with an axe. He had done this in revenge because Sir Arthur had sacked him from his public service job. Manning's face was left so badly scarred that he retired from public life to the isolation of what was then quiet rural Milton House.

Cordelia Bowerman took the watercolour 'home' to England with her. For over a century her father-in-law's painting, the first dated and signed record of Brisbane's convict era, lay hidden until one of Cordelia's descendants found it in 1981 among some old postcards and engravings. Hoping that the painting would be of some value the finder sent it to Christie's of South Kensington, London asking them to sell it. The cataloguer, unaware that the Moreton Bay Settlement was the early name for Brisbane and that the painting was a vital part of the city's heritage, put a low reserve on it.

The author, Susanna de Vries, saw the watercolour catalogued as *Panorama of the Moreton Bay Settlement*, bid for the painting and acquired it. And so this historic watercolour returned to Brisbane more than a century after the artist had painted it. When Susanna's marriage to the late Dr Larry Evans was dissolved the painting was donated to the John Oxley Library under the tax incentive scheme and became one of the library's treasures.

The initials H.W.B.B., which appear on the original drawing, are clearly those of Commissariat Officer Henry William Boucher Bowerman.

Bowerman was born in London in 1794. After a short training as a topographical artist, he joined the Commissariat Service and was in charge of the Commissariat Store of the Moreton Bay Settlement from 1830 to 1835. He died at sea in 1836 off the coast of Victoria.

From Bowerman's delicate yet detailed panorama, showing the everyday life of the penal colony, it is possible to trace the evolution of North Quay, William and Queen Streets.

The painting shows how a penal colony, ten thousand miles from Britain, used elements of English Georgian style architecture in its building design, which were not very suitable for Queensland's subtropical climate.

The small Georgian style cottages along North Quay were meticulously drawn by Henry Boucher Bowerman.

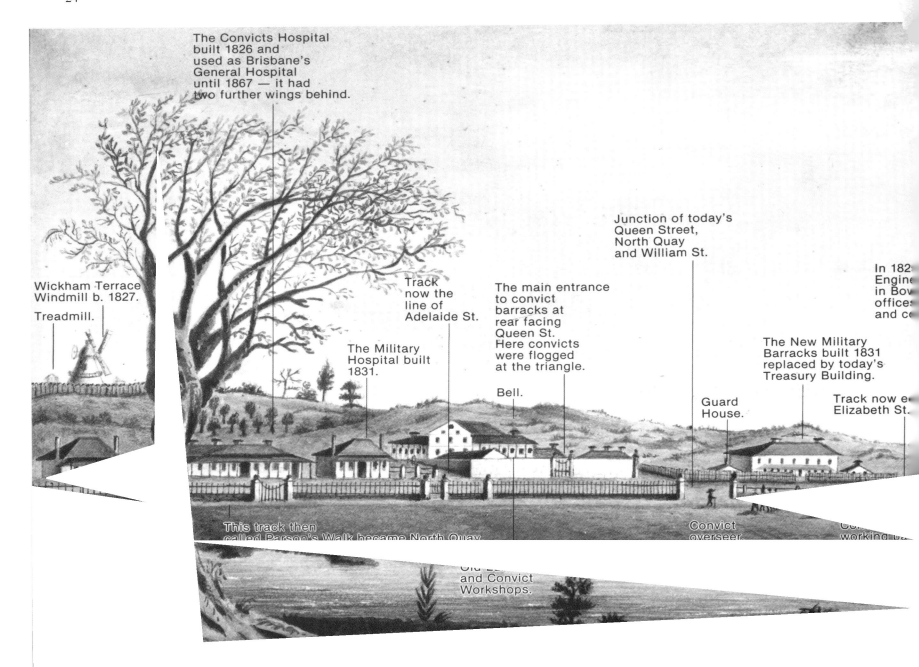

Plate 17. THE MORETON BAY SETTLEMENT, NEW SOUTH WALES IN 1835 by HENRY WILLIAM BOUCHER BOWERMAN.
Panorama drawn from South Brisbane, from the site of today's South Bank Cultural Centre. Pen and grisaille wash drawing, heightened with white. Initialled H.W.B.B. fecit [made] 3.5.35.

Plan of Brisbane in 1844

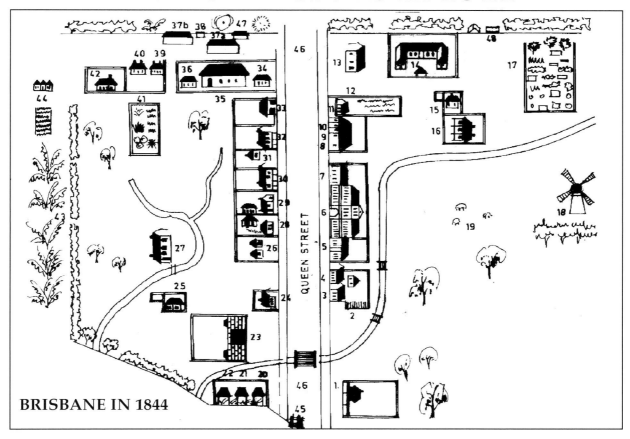

Plate 18 A plan drawn by C F. Gerler in March 1886. Gerler arrived from Germany in 1844 to assist the missionaries at Nundah. His drawing is out of scale. A photograph of Gerler's original plan is in E.J.T. Barton, 'Jubilee History of Queensland', 1910, and has here been re-drawn by Jake de Vries.

Legend [edited and adapted to the above re-drawn plan]

1. Andrew Petrie's home
2. Handel, cattle drover
3. Savory [the only baker]
4. Bensteads, sawyers
5. T. Richardson [Wool and General Store]
   From the bricks of this old house the first Wesleyan Church was built.
6. Convict Barracks [later Court House]
7. W. Kent [druggist shop]
8. Fitzpatrick [the first Chief Constable]
9. The Lock-up
10. The Constables' Place
11. Slates' Post Office [old]
12. Slates' Pineapple Garden
13. Church of England
14. The Hospital
15. Mort, the milkman
16. Wright's Hotel
17. The General Cemetery
18. Treadmill and Windmill
19. Edmonston's sheep for slaughter
20. Richard Jones
21. Dr Simpson [the first Commissioner]
22. Old Major Prior
23. The Gaol
24. Skyring's Beehives [soft goods shop]
25. Hayes, the milkman
26. Brothers Fraser [first houses]
27. The Catholic Church
28. McLean's Blacksmith's Shop
29. Edmontston's [the only butcher]
30. Bow's Hotel
31. Taylor Shappart
32. Montifleur [a financier]
33. W. Pickering [now Bank of N.S.W.]
34. Sergeant Jones
35. Soldiers' Barracks
36. Officer De Winton
37. Commissariat Store
38. Queen's Wharf [the only one]
39. Captain Wickham's Office
40. Commissioner T. Kent
41. The Commissioner's Garden
42. Captain Coley's cottage
43. Government Gardens
44. Father Hanley [the only Priest]
45. Sawpits [later Gas Works]
46. Queen Street
47. The Boat House and Boatman's House
48. The first Burial Place [two graves]

The Hospital and Surgeon's Cottage

The long, low building, shown on the government plan as the Convict Hospital [plate 19], was built by order of Captain Patrick Logan as part of the Moreton Bay Convict Settlement. The hospital was built on North Quay near the corner of Queen Street. It had a grim reputation as a place where many patients died.

The settlement's death rate was higher than that of any other penal settlement in Australia. In addition to malnutrition and diseases brought in from the tropics, at least one convict death, caused by infected wounds from severe flogging, has been recorded.

It was one of the grimmer duties of the Resident Surgeon to be present at the floggings, which took place at the wooden triangle set up on Queen Street, outside the Convict Barracks.

A young Scottish squatter on the Darling Downs named Ernest Dalrymple was brought down by bullock dray from his property, desperately ill with tuberculosis. After a painful journey he was told that there were no available beds in the Convict Hospital, where even after free settlement assigned convict labourers were treated. Dalrymple was taken to a Brisbane hotel, where he died.

Brisbane desperately needed a larger hospital. But even after Queensland became a separate colony there was still no money to build a larger hospital. All Government building plans were frozen and it took eight years to raise enough money to build the Bowen Hospital, now part of the Royal Brisbane Hospital.

The Surgeon's cottage on North Quay was built in Georgian colonial style in 1831, by order of Governor Darling. It provided accommodation for the Resident Surgeon and his family. With its steeply pitched roof and overhanging verandahs, the cottage was cool in summer, catching the breeze from the river. The Georgian-style sash windows in the cottage and the Convict Hospital were fitted with latticed shutters. To the rear of the cottage was a small enclosed verandah and stables for the horse that had been made available to the surgeon by his employer, the Government of New South Wales.

The Surgeon's residence was convict-built. It had thick brick walls, high ceilings and hand-made cedar doors and window frames, made by convict carpenters. It is sad that this residence and other convict-built cottages in the settlement, as well as the first home of Andrew Petrie [plate 2], were demolished. Fortunately, similar cottages have been preserved in New South Wales and Tasmania, examples being those on Goat Island in Sydney Harbour and in the Rocks area of Sydney.

Dr David Ballow lived in this cottage from 1838 to 1850 and provided medical services to a population of pioneering free settlers. At that time the sewers were often open drains, attracting swarms of flies. Typhoid, jaundice and dysentery, as well as other life-threatening tropical diseases, were prevalent. Dr Ballow worked unceasingly for his patients but died of lice-born typhus while still a relatively young man.

Plate 19.   FRONT ELEVATIONS OF THE SURGEON'S QUARTERS AND THE CONVICT HOSPITAL, erected in 1826.
From plan 31 [1840], Moreton Bay Plans, Queensland State Archives.

Plate 20. BRISBANE'S FIRST HOSPITAL ON NORTH QUAY. Pencil sketch by LADY ELIZA HODGSON, made c. 1850 when this hospital served Brisbane Town and the Darling Downs. The hospital, built by convicts in 1826 is shown on the right, while to the left is the Georgian colonial cottage used by the Surgeon. The hospital's ceilings were found to be too low, so in many later buildings the ceilings were raised.

Reproduced courtesy of a private collection in Britain.

Two Colonial Houses of the 1840s

Newstead House

Newstead House was the first large private home in Brisbane. Newstead derives from the Scottish word 'stead' meaning a large farm. Newstead House, with walls of plastered brick, was built around 1844 by Patrick Leslie. Patrick's wife Kate, a grand-daughter of Philip Gidley King, personally supervised the lay-out of the garden, where they grew grape vines, banana palms, roses, jasmine, honeysuckle and ivy. Newstead Cottage, as it was then known, was a self-sufficient but isolated paradise, where melons, pineapples, cucumbers, wheat, corn and barley grew. Barley was for their horses, cattle, ducks and pigeons. In a letter dated April 1845, addressed to his father in Scotland, Patrick Leslie wrote:

> We called the place Newstead since Watty [his young brother Walter Leslie] liked the name so much. The windows of the Cottage [sic] look out over the garden and upriver to a most magnificent reach and there is a through draught which in summer is delightful. Behind

Plate 21. NEWSTEAD HOUSE, BRISBANE, 1853. Watercolour by LORD HENRY SCOTT. This unsigned painting returned to England with the artist.

Mitchell Library, Sydney.

the Cottage [sic] we have a detached cooking place, where we cook in hot weather and keep all fires out of the house, together with a saddle room, a wash-house and a water shed under which the water casks stand.

Two years later Patrick Leslie sold Newstead House for £1,000 to his brother-in-law, Police Magistrate John Wickham. The sale enabled Patrick Leslie to move up to the Darling Downs to help his brother, whose stock was by now overloading the Canning Downs property. He also had to manage his own property Goomburra.

Captain John Wickham and his wife Anna extended Newstead House and added the verandahs shown in the picture. They also replaced the wall between the Leslies' sitting room and bedroom with folding cedar doors. The room could be used as a ballroom so that Newstead became Brisbane's first unofficial Government House.

Captain John Wickham, Police Magistrate and Queen's representative for the Moreton Bay area, was the key man in town when Lord Henry Scott, son of the Duke of Buccleuch and Queensberry, visited Brisbane.

Wickham had the role of surrogate governor in a town that still was part of northern New South Wales. He was also a seafarer and explorer of repute, having been second-in-command on the *Beagle* on its voyage with Charles Darwin and Conrad Martens. He had also led a marine survey of Moreton Bay and North Australia.

John Wickham and the Scottish settlers Patrick and George Leslie were related by marriage, having all married daughters of Hannibal Hayes Macarthur of Sydney's Parramatta. In the 1840s, Newstead House was the centre of social life of the new town of Brisbane and the Darling Downs, home of the 'Grass Dukes of the Downs'. John and Anna Wickham entertained the squatters at balls and supper parties under the light of hundreds of candles.

Sadly, Anna Wickham died of consumption. When Lord Henry Scott paid a visit to Newstead House, widowed Captain Wickham was living there alone with an elderly housekeeper. The small figure standing on the verandah in Lord Henry's watercolour could be John Wickham himself, waiting to welcome Lord Henry, who was on a world tour with his tutor.

Bulimba House

Bulimba House was built by the construction firm of Andrew Petrie. Gradually a number of timber cottages were erected around it.

Bulimba is an aboriginal word meaning 'place of the magpie-larks' also known as peewits. Here Scottish pastoralist David McConnel bought acres of uncleared land at a bend in the river, known to the Aborigines as Toogoolawah. McConnel employed Scottish labourers to clear the land. They built small homes for themselves, planted maize and helped building Bulimba House.

On 1 June 1850, the *Moreton Bay Courier* described Bulimba House as 'a capacious mansion of Brisbane sandstone in course of erection'.

David McConnel's young wife Mary was one of the first free European women living in Brisbane. At that time medical services were limited. Brisbane's only adult hospital refused to admit children under five, with the result that Mary's baby son died. Mary raised the money to found the Brisbane Children's Hospital, arranged for a fully trained matron to come out from London and paid the matron's fare and salary herself.

Plate 22. BULIMBA HOUSE in 1851. A pencil drawing by Conrad Martens.
John Oxley Library, State Library of Queensland.

The Three Villages of Old Brisbane

South Brisbane and Kangaroo Point regarded themselves as entirely separate from the more prosperous area across the river, then called North Brisbane. Linked to North Brisbane was the settlement of Fortitude Valley and beyond that lay the separate German missionary settlement of Nundah.

Together these settlements formed the most northerly town of New South Wales. In the 1840s Brisbane was a remote outpost that initially developed relatively slowly. In 1846 the town's population consisted of 1,220 men and 477 women and by 1851 it had 2,543 inhabitants. But by 1864 the population had increased to 12,551.

In North Brisbane land could cost as much as £100 an acre for choicer central blocks while south of the Brisbane River land cost only £1 an acre. Many people predicted that North Brisbane would become the capital of the new state of Queensland once it achieved independence from New South Wales.

South Brisbane

Young squatter George Knight Fairholme drew the separate village of South Brisbane in 1845, when the combined populations of South Brisbane *and* Kangaroo Point amounted to only 346 inhabitants.

At that time, South Brisbane had an entirely different atmosphere to North Brisbane and was described by one of the early settlers as having 'the tang of the stock-whip

Plate 23.   WILLIAM STREET AND SOUTH BRISBANE IN 1845, after GEORGE KNIGHT ERSKINE FAIRHOLME.
Hand-coloured engraving initialled G.K.E.F. and dated 1845. See also Owen Stanley's painting [plate 29].
Mitchell Library, Sydney.

and the bullock yoke'. The south side of the river was a frontier settlement, a tough area of taverns, brothels and wharves. The wool clippers were not allowed to use the Government Wharf on Queens Wharf Road so had to anchor in the middle of the river or moor themselves to the large tree, shown in the centre of George Fairholme's picture, on land owned by an avaricious Scotsman named McIntire who demanded money for this facility.

All transit between the three separate villages had to be made by the Kangaroo Point or Russell Street ferries or by rowing boat. Fairholme used to travel down from the Darling Downs to South Brisbane with a loaded bullock dray bringing wool bales to be shipped overseas. By 1850 South Brisbane had five wharves. In June of that year *Moreton Bay Courier* described it as having 'cottages sprinkled here and there along the bank'.

Brisbane's warehouses charged relatively high storage rates, sometimes holding squatters to ransom for more money. To avoid paying storage charges to warehouse owners, squatters and drovers often waited for days near South Brisbane's wharves until a clipper arrived and their wool could be loaded.

South Brisbane, with easier access to Ipswich and the Darling Downs, had pubs, boarding houses, brothels, a church and a library for the convenience of squatters, bullock drovers and jackeroos, the 'wild Colonial boys'.

South Brisbane's residents were mainly storekeepers, publicans, owners of 'sly-grog shops', prostitutes, ferrymen, boat-builders, speculators and dealers in land. The settlement had a Wild West frontier flavour with drunken men brawling in the streets.

In the 1850s Mary McConnel of Bulimba described how 'much business is being done with Ipswich and the bush so that South Brisbane is becoming a busy place'.

Squatters like Fairholme rode down to South Brisbane, bronzed from working on their properties. Mounted on thoroughbred horses they carried pistols in their holsters and shot-guns in their saddle-bags. After all, South Brisbane could be dangerous to reach as desperadoes, or convicts turned bushrangers, could lie in wait to rob drovers and other travellers of their money.

Kangaroo Point Village, 1845

Like South Brisbane, Kangaroo Point was separated from North Brisbane by the river and could be reached only by ferry or rowing boat from North Brisbane.

The first sale of Kangaroo Point land took place in December 1843. George Fairholme was a frequent visitor to Kangaroo Point once it had been declared 'open to settlers and free persons'.

Fairholme's pen and ink sketch of pioneering days at Kangaroo Point was drawn from the far side of the Brisbane River. It shows the convict-built windmill on Wickham Terrace with its sails still in place. But his view is far from accurate. The hills are shown much higher than they really are, probably drawn that way to impress relatives back home in Scotland.

When George Fairholme made this sketch he was working on South Toolburra Station. He visited Brisbane several times a year to collect his mail, sell wool and engage newly arrived immigrants to work on the Station.

In Fairholme's day Kangaroo Point consisted of slab and weatherboard cottages, hotels like Sutton's Inn and the Bush Inn, patronised by slaughtermen and timber workers. Numerous sly-grog shops served as gambling dens and brothels, catering for the needs of the lusty young seamen and squatters. Wild alcoholic parties were young men's compensation for weeks spent at sea, for working long hours in the slaughterhouse, run by 'Tinker' Campbell, or for weeks spent in isolated logging camps out in the bush.

Many Indigenous people came to Kangaroo Point and an extract from the *Moreton Bay Courier*, dated 16 October 1847 relates how

> the natives of Kangaroo Point daily procure immense quantities of delicious prawns, which abound near Kangaroo Point in our splendid river and they dispose of five or six quarts of these to the inhabitants in return for a loaf of bread or a small piece of tobacco.

Plate 24. KANGAROO POINT, BRISBANE after GEORGE KNIGHT ERSKINE FAIRHOLME. *Hand-coloured engraving after an original pen and ink sketch made c. 1845, printed in an undated book in a limited edition, circulated to the artist's family and friends titled* **'Fifteen Views in Australia by G.K.E.F.'**. *An historically important picture of early Brisbane life, it shows the first houses and bush inns built after the area was opened up to free settlement. The population of Brisbane in 1846 was 1,220 men and 477 women and the separate villages of North and South Brisbane and Kangaroo Point had only 255 buildings. The cows, pigs and sheep of the first settlers grazed freely along the riverbanks and later wharves and warehouses would be built there. George Fairholme would eventually leave the Darling Downs and buy the property of 'Bromelton' from Thomas Murray-Prior.*

Mitchell Library, Sydney.

Kangaroo Point expands

Another view of the pioneer settlement of Kangaroo Point was engraved in 1874 by the English artist J.C. Armytage. Ironically, the artist never visited Brisbane. He engraved his view of Kangaroo Point from a photograph supplied to him by Richard Daintree, Agent-General for Queensland. The engraving [plate 25] is one of the pictures Armytage produced for an illustrated book written by the author Edwin Carton Booth, intended to encourage emigration to Australia.

Armytage's view depicts the tip of Kangaroo Point from across the Brisbane River and shows it largely as a working class area. The simple timber cottages shown in the picture often replaced slab huts with bark roofs.

Many of the first timber dwellings had brick chimneys and separate kitchens to prevent fire. Inside they were very primitive indeed, with dirt or 'ant bed' floors. Running water or drains were lacking. They had outdoor dunnies emptied by nightsoil collectors using 'honey-carts', which were insanitary and could cause disease. Most of the cottages had fowl-runs, vegetable gardens, nut and fruit trees such as banana, lemon, orange and paw-paw. The larger yards had bunya pines, Moreton Bay fig trees, camphor laurel or mango trees. The latter attracted flying foxes that rustled and squawked among the leaves at night.

Kangaroo Point had [and still has] a ferry connection with North Brisbane. The ferry arrived close to the steps of the first Customs House, known as the 'new Customs House' completed in 1850 on a site adjacent to the Queens Wharf. As Brisbane's ferries were considered relatively expensive for a working man, some people living at Kangaroo Point built or bought rowing boats, which they moored near their homes.

In the foreground of J.C. Armytage's engraving two men row their goods between Kangaroo Point and New Farm, while various small craft are anchored close to the riverbank.

Besides the Kangaroo Point ferry were boiling-down works managed by the entrepreneurial 'Tinker' Campbell, and owned by Scottish pastoralist Evan Mackenzie [1816–1883], owner of Kilcoy during the wool depression of 1841–44. At this time the price of wool fell dramatically and bankrupted many squatters.

In the depression the squatters needed to sell their sheep to repay start-up loans from their families in Britain or from Scottish banks. The supply of unwanted sheep and cattle far exceeded the market for their meat.

In 1843 a group of Darling Downs squatters persuaded Evan Mackenzie to establish the Kangaroo Point boiling-down works and a private wharf to service them. In these boiling-down works sheep and cattle were stunned with an axe, beheaded, skinned, the haunches chopped up for consumption and the rest thrown into huge iron vats which held up to 24 bullocks or three times that number of sheep. The fat was boiled out, poured into casks and became tallow. The casks were shipped to England to make soap and candles.

Unfortunately, large amounts of blood, offal and other grisly remains produced from the boiling-down works drained into gutters and then into the Brisbane River, causing considerable pollution problems. Sharks were attracted upriver by the blood and offal. The foul stench that hung over the whole area was almost unbearable.

The abandoned buildings of Campbell's Tallow Works lay idle once the prices of wool and beef recovered. Higher prices for wool led to a general reluctance on the part of the squatters to send their sheep and cattle to the boiling-down works, causing unemployment for the workers, who had to search for other sources of income.

When the wool price lifted employment was found in the wool trade and at the shipping wharves. Land at Kangaroo Point became gradually more expensive as confidence returned. Those making good money from the wool trade built substantial houses at Kangaroo Point.

In June 1850, the *Moreton Bay Courier* described how 'at Kangaroo Point many new houses have lately been built, and here the bustle and activity usually observable at the shipping wharf, gives the first indications of the commerce of Brisbane.'

After Queensland separated from New South Wales Kangaroo Point became a thriving place. Sadly, the area was devastated by the 1893 flood, which swept many of the timber cottages away or damaged them badly.

Plate 25. *LOOKING ACROSS KANGAROO POINT FROM BOWEN TERRACE TO PARLIAMENT HOUSE AND THE BOTANIC GARDENS after J. C. ARMYTAGE. Engraved by the artist on steel, published in 1874. It shows Kangaroo Point as a small rural community with Main Street as its only road. The Queensland gold rush was just starting and ships which had brought the eager prospectors to Brisbane can be seen moored at the Town Reach.*

Private collection.

Trained Artists visit Brisbane Town

Conrad Martens

Conrad Martens [1801–1878] was, arguably, Australia's greatest artist of the mid nineteenth century and the only major colonial professional painter to depict Brisbane.

Before arriving in Australia, Martens had served as a ship's artist on *The Beagle*, participating in a scientific expedition exploring and charting the coast of South America. He sailed around Cape Horn and on arrival in Australia settled in Sydney. Here, during the wool boom of the 1830s, he found wealthy clients for his paintings, married a Sydney girl and built himself a house.

The depression years of the mid-1840s saw Martens, with a young family to support, desperately searching for new markets. The developing area of Brisbane and the pastoral properties of the Darling Downs seemed to offer hope of fresh clients. Martens had a good friend in Brisbane, Captain James Wickham, Chief Magistrate, who lived in style at Newstead House. John Wickham had served as a lieutenant aboard *The Beagle*, where he had met Martens, the artist to the expedition, and Charles Darwin, its naturalist. Martens and Wickham had stayed in touch with each other and their old shipmate Charles Darwin.

Martens sailed to Brisbane aboard the ship *Toroa* and arrived on Friday 7 November 1851, passing New Farm and North Brisbane on the right and Bulimba and Kangaroo Point on the left. The ship berthed at the only wharf in South Brisbane, shown by artist Owen Stanley in his view of Brisbane in 1848 [plate 29]. *The Moreton Bay Courier* announced that:

> Martens intends to make sketches of the scenery in this district. Mr Martens will find ample space for the exercise of his pencil in delineating the beautiful views presented from various points on the banks of the Brisbane River.

During his sixteen-day stay in Brisbane Martens did just that. His first pencil drawing was made on 7 November. It depicted a weatherboard cottage at New Farm owned by the once wealthy merchant Richard Jones, who had moved north from Sydney after suffering losses in the wool depression. Martens made another view [plate 26] on 12 November 1851. It shows the straggle of free-

Plate 26.
VIEW OF BRISBANE TOWN, 12 Nov 1851.
Pencil sketch by CONRAD MARTENS

Mitchell Library, Sydney.

standing cottages that lined the unpaved track that would later develop into Queen Street. A small gully, which became a creek when flooded, divides the drawing. On the far right we see the area between today's Edward and Adelaide Streets and the cottage and outbuilding owned by blacksmith and wheelwright Thomas Fitzsimmons. A pair of bullocks can be seen outside the premises. Unfortunately for Martens, Fitzsimmons did not commission a painting of his workshop from him.

The sketch below titled *North and South Brisbane* shows a ship lying at anchor at South Brisbane which could be the *Toroa*, the ship that brought Martens as its only passenger to Brisbane. On the opposite side of the river are the former Government Gardens, part of the old Moreton Bay Settlement where free settlers were now allowed to graze their cattle and saplings were planted so it could become the City Botanic Gardens.

Martens spent 16 days in Brisbane, making several pencil drawings. His stay has been documented by Dr John Steele in his book *Conrad Martens in Queensland* and by Susanna de Vries in *Conrad Martens on The Beagle and in Australia*.

Martens kept an account book in which he wrote down the names of everyone who commissioned watercolours from him and it shows that the hard-headed shopkeepers of Queen Street and the tavern keepers of South Brisbane and Kangaroo Point did not want to part with money for paintings of Brisbane Town, considering art an unnecessary extravagance.

Martens' best patron for his Brisbane watercolours was an educated young Darling Downs squatter named Henry Stuart Russell, who was having a house built at Kangaroo Point. Russell called the house Ravenscott, later renamed Shafston House, of which Martens made several views.

Plate 27.   NORTH AND SOUTH BRISBANE FROM THE BRISBANE ROCKS, KANGAROO POINT, by CONRAD MARTENS. *Pencil drawing, signed and dated 18 November 1851. The picture shows the wharves and houses at Stanley Quay along the South Brisbane Reach. Shown across the Town Reach is Queen Street, still a bullock track fringed by a few small houses and shops, while cattle graze in what became the city Botanic Gardens.*

Detail of a drawing held in the collection of the Queensland Art Gallery.

At that time Kangaroo Point consisted of very basic workers' cottages with steeply pitched roofs plus a few expensive homes. Main Street, lying along the crest of the ridge, was the only proper street in the area; the rest were dirt tracks. The two-storey house at the end of Main Street is Silverwells, an historic Kangaroo Point home and the oldest surviving residential building on the Point. The house was built of stone, quarried on Kangaroo Point for Evan Mackenzie, who purchased land here very cheaply indeed in 1840, the era of government land sales.

The home in the centre of the picture below, facing Mr Thornton's house, was built in colonial style for James Warner, who had been appointed as Government Surveyor. James Warner had been sent to Brisbane in 1829 to help Andrew Petrie prepare detailed plans of the city area, so that the land could be subdivided into blocks for forthcoming government land sales.

During his visit, Conrad Martens made various pencil sketches of the Brisbane River and the Colonial houses overlooking it. He spent a sunny morning drawing Kangaroo Point from the verandah of Colonel Thornton's home.

Thornton, a retired colonel, worked at the time for Brisbane's first Customs Office. His home in Eagle Street was near the Customs House where he worked as a 'Tide

Plate 28. KANGAROO POINT, DRAWN FROM THE HOME OF MR THORNTON IN EAGLE STREET by CONRAD MARTENS. *Pencil sketch, heightened with white in the typical Martens' style. Signed lower right and dated November 22, 1851.*

Mitchell Library, Sydney.

Waiter' as Customs Inspectors were known. Thornton's name is still commemorated in Thornton Street, Kangaroo Point.

A view of Kangaroo Point was commissioned from Martens by Scottish-born George Leslie, a grazier on the Darling Downs. After George Leslie's death, his widow Emmeline [born Macarthur] married a Danish-born Naval officer. Marten's paintings, including the view of Kangaroo Point, remained with her heirs in England until some were sold at an auction held by Sotheby's in London in October 1980. The most important Martens watercolour for Brisbane, showing the Brisbane River, was later re-sold by Christie's Auctioneers to the Queensland Art Gallery. Smaller views of the Darling Downs, including *Forest, Cunningham's Gap*, were bought by the Queensland Art Gallery direct from Emmeline's descendants.

Martens made several views of the meandering Brisbane River, including one painted for Lord Henry Scott [front cover and plate 31] and a variant version painted for George Leslie. The Leslie view, dated 1855 [plate 30], was made from Martens' original pencil sketch of 1851 and shows a ferry taking livestock across the river. Comparing the Lord Henry Scott view with the one painted for George Leslie shows how Martens varied the trees and vines in the foreground and replaced the horse ferry with a dinghy with a red sail.

Lord Henry Scott took Martens' views of Brisbane and several of Sydney Harbour back to England. His direct descendant, the present Lord Montagu of Beaulieu, sold the paintings to the National Library of Australia in the 1980s.

In 1862 Martens made another painting of North Brisbane from Kangaroo Point and the Brisbane River as a present for his old shipmate, Charles Darwin. The picture was intended as a gift to congratulate Darwin on the publication of his book *On the Origin of Species by Means of Natural Selection*. The painting also gave Darwin some idea of Brisbane, the place where their old *Beagle* shipmate John Wickham worked as Government Resident and Magistrate. Leonard Darwin donated the watercolour to the Queensland Art Gallery in 1913. It shows the Convict Windmill and a distant glimpse of the Convict Barracks. The paper has now deteriorated so badly and it cannot be restored successfully.

Owen Stanley at Moreton Bay

Like Conrad Martens, Captain Owen Stanley, R.N. [1811–1850], was a man who loved the sea and ships and who had a keen eye for observation. Owen Stanley was paid by the Navy to conduct surveys and made watercolours as a hobby, while for Martens painting was the only means of support. Stanley's watercolours are rare. Some were used to illustrate *Discoveries in Australia* by Captain John Lort Stokes.

En route to Cape York, Captain Stanley and his ship HMS *Rattlesnake* arrived in Brisbane late 1847 and he stayed there during the early part of 1848. He conducted a survey of Moreton Bay aboard the ship *Bramble*, which he painted during a storm over the bay. Extant paintings include *Breakfast Creek–at Captain Wickham's*, a view from Bishopsbourne [private collection] and *Pilot Station, Amity Point*, signed and dated 1847 [Mitchell Library]. The latter view shows a lone Aborigine, wearing a red shirt and holding a spear, standing beside the pilot's isolated timber cottage.

This view of South Brisbane in 1847–48 [Plate 29] was recently discovered among the collections of the National Library and authenticated by Susanna de Vries and Dr John Steele. This important watercolour, painted from the corner of Alice and William Streets, shows the development of what was then known as Stanley Quay [now South Bank].

In 1848, the Australian Steam Navegation Company bought two allotments on Stanley Quay and built a wharf which they later extended. North and South Brisbane were vying with each other for commerical supremacy. In 1859 the A.S.N Company moved its offices across the river and would eventually make Naldham House [now the Polo Club] their headquarters. Other merchants and traders hedged their bets by operating on both sides of the Brisbane River.

Plate 29. SOUTH BRISBANE [NEAR THE CORNER OF ALICE AND WILLIAM STREETS]. Watercolour by OWEN STANLEY, 1847–48.
It shows the A.S.N. Company's wharf on Stanley Quay [today's South Bank] with its primitive bush inns, houses of ill repute, shops and private homes. Two decades later many more warehouses would line the riverfront. The slopes of Mount Coot-tha [somewhat enlarged to make a better painting] can be seen on the skyline. This view, purchased by the wealthy collector Rex NanKivell in London, was titled *Harris's Wharf and South Brisbane*, erroneously dated 1868 and was attributed to another artist. In the course of research for this book it was discovered to be by Owen Stanley, painted two decades earlier. The watercolour is rare because there are very few paintings of Brisbane of this period.

Rex NanKivell Collection, National Library of Australia, Canberra.

Plate 30. BRISBANE AND KANGAROO POINT FROM BOWEN TERRACE, 1855. *Watercolour by* CONRAD MARTENS. *This view, although dated 1855, was made from the sketch Martens drew in Brisbane on his 1851 visit. It is the only one of Martens' Brisbane paintings to show the ferry, powered by steam, that transported horses and other livestock as well as people across the Brisbane River. Painted for the Leslie family, by descent to Jane de Falbe, sold by Sotheby's and then by Christie's and now owned by the Queensland Art Gallery.*

Photographed at Christie's pre-sale viewing. © *Pandanus Press.*

Plate 31. BRISBANE RIVER WITH VIEW OF BRISBANE TOWN AND KANGAROO POINT, 1852. *Watercolour by* CONRAD MARTENS. *The windmill on Wickham Terrace appears on the right hand side of the skyline; the wharves and a number of buildings of North Brisbane are visible while Kangaroo Point is largely undeveloped. Martens emphasises the bush surrounding this small frontier town.*

National Library of Australia, Canberra.

Plate 32. BRISBANE IN 1851, SHOWING PETRIE BIGHT AND EAGLE STREET FROM KANGAROO POINT by CONRAD MARTENS. *Detail of a watercolour, signed and dated 1852, painted from a pencil sketch [now lost] made the previous year during Martens' visit to Brisbane. Martens shows the first small Customs House at Petrie Bight with Andrew Petrie's Wharf Street home just above it. Along the waterfront stands John Richardson's three-storey Wool and Trading Store. The painting shows the windmill on the skyline and virgin bush that in 1851 still covered the area between Adelaide Street and Wickham Terrace.*

Mitchell Library, Sydney.

The 'Old' and the 'New' Customs House

Brisbane's first Customs House on Petrie Bight, had just been built when Conrad Martens showed it in one of the paintings he made during his 1851 visit [plate 32].

Brisbane's first small single-storey Customs House was built on the same site as the present Customs House and opened for business in 1850. Adjacent to it was John Richardson's huge Wool and Trading Store, built along what would become Eagle Street.

The first Customs House was built by the construction firm of Andrew Petrie. His eldest son, John [1822–1892], had become a partner in the business in 1843.

Martens' painting, based on a pencil drawing he made in 1851, is historically important and shows a riverside pioneering settlement encircled by tree-covered slopes.

The Windmill, by that time shorn of its sails, is silhouetted against the evening sky and land along Eagle Street is still covered with virgin bush. By that time large riverfront blocks had been bought at auction by Dr Stephen Simpson of Wolston House, the first Commissioner of Crown Lands for Moreton Bay. The land to the left of Dr Simpson's property, near today's Elizabeth and Eagle Streets, was leased by Dr David Ballow.

Conrad Martens shows a small ferry crossing the river at roughly the same spot where, a century and a half later, a ferry still operates.

The adjacent photograph shows the far more imposing Customs House, which replaced the one-storey building in 1889. By the late 19th century a larger Customs House was needed to cope with all the paperwork from ships that arrived or departed. By now Brisbane had become a trading centre of wharves and warehouses where customs' dues were an important source of revenue. This is reflected in the scale and grandeur of the present Customs House, built to cope with increased shipping in the rapidly expanding capital city of the new colony.

The Customs House was designed by Charles McLay [1860–1918], a quiet Scot who worked as a draftsman in the Colonial Architect's Office. He surprised everyone by winning the competition to design the building. Familiar with the neoclassical buildings of Edinburgh, McLay's classically inspired edifice took three years to erect and was completed in 1889. It has two handsome facades and a copper-clad dome. It now operates as an art gallery, function centre and restaurant under the aegis of the University of Queensland.

Plate 33. BRISBANE'S SECOND CUSTOMS HOUSE. A recent photograph taken from Kangaroo Point.

© Pandanus Press.

Pioneers of the Fortitude Valley

The Fortitude Valley was originally known as 'Bell's Valley', after Lieutenant Bell of the Moreton Bay Garrison, who allegedly protested against the severe floggings meted out to convicts. During the early 1850s, it changed its name from Bell's Valley to Fortitude Valley.

Scotland's Reverend Dr John Dunmore Lang had visited the Brisbane area in 1847 and thought it suitable for cotton growing. His extensive lecture tours and offer of free land fired the imagination of over a thousand British Presbyterians, who arrived on the migrant ships the *Fortitude*, the *Chasely*, and the *Lima* in January 1849.

The migrants believed that under Dr Lang's privately-sponsored scheme, the Government of New South Wales [under whose jurisdiction Brisbane still lay] would give them substantial grants of land suitable for growing cotton. Nettled by what they saw as Dr Lang's high-handed actions, the British Government, which so far had not sent any sponsored free settlers to Brisbane, rushed to dispatch 240 English men and women to Moreton Bay aboard the barque *Artemisia*. The Government-funded migrants arrived a month ahead of Lang's sponsored migrants and were housed and fed by the Colonial Government. They soon found employment in Brisbane or on the Darling Downs.

Unfortunately, the *Fortitude* settlers became victims of the fact that Lang's promises for assistance from the Colonial Office in London had not been confirmed in writing. Lang's abrasive personality had made him powerful enemies in the British and Colonial governments. Earl Grey, as Colonial Secretary, disliked Lang and denied all knowledge of promises to help Lang's migrants and instructed the Colonial Government to give the migrants no assistance whatever.

Colonial authorities therefore refused all help so some of these hapless migrants had to camp out at Bulimba, at Petrie Bight or in Bell's Valley. They had to sleep in tents made of old sheets while they built themselves bark and slab huts until they had jobs and could afford something better. At the time 'Bell's Valley' was considered undesirable and even dangerous due to the risk of attack by Aborigines, who were annoyed at being displaced from what they regarded as their land.

Diggles' drawing shows the Valley soon after it had been cleared of trees, scrub and vines. Although still sparsely inhabited at the time, blocks of land had been sold to investors and settlers from 1845 onwards.

On the left of Ann Street, at the top of the hill, we can see the steeply-pitched roof of Adderton, home of Dr George Fullerton, which in 1863 was purchased by the Sisters of Mercy for their new All Hallows' School. Below it lies the Fortitude Valley Denominational School used by Presbyterian settlers, which had opened the year before Diggles made his pencil drawing. Just below the school was a creek, which originated on the slopes of Spring Hill and gave its name to Water Street. On the top of the hill to the right is the house called Darra, which was later demolished to build the Holy Name Cathedral opposite the future All Hallows' School.

Plate 34. ANN STREET [S.W. VIEW] FORTITUDE VALLEY, 1858 by SYLVESTER DIGGLES. Pencil sketch looking towards the city near today's Valley Post Office.

Queensland Art Gallery.

The First Exhibition or 'Ekka' 1876

Brisbane hummed with excitement on Tuesday 22 August 1876, the occasion of the very first 'Ekka'. Unfortunately an unexpectedly hot day jammed the new brass turnstiles which slowed the admittance of some 15,000 people to a trickle. *The Queenslander* described a somewhat chaotic start to what has become a Brisbane institution.

> By eleven o'clock an immense throng was pouring along Gregory Terrace. Outside a large crowd awaited the arrival of Governor, Sir William Wellington Cairns. The heat was considerable for the time of the year. One cadet who had been standing to attention for more than an hour was overpowered by the heat: he was removed in a fainting condition to the refreshment building. After the Governor made a speech declaring the Exhibition open, the National Anthem was played. The first gun of an Artillery salute boomed out from Victoria Park and was answered by a prodigious clamour — five steam engines shrieking and whistling and the crowd cheering. Meanwhile the band of the Fire Brigade struck up. The resulting clamour was anything but favourable to a respectful hearing of Mr. Brunton Stephens' patriotic poem.

The drawing below shows the exhibition grounds from the site of today's Royal Brisbane Hospital with the Fortitude Valley in the background. The large timber building in the centre was destroyed by fire in 1888. It was replaced by a brick building, which later became the site of the old Queensland Museum [plates 57 and 58].

Plate 35.   BIRD'S-EYE VIEW OF QUEENSLAND EXHIBITION, BOWEN PARK, 1876. Published in the Supplement of 'The Week', dated September 1876.

Significant Buildings of the 1860s & 1870s

Parliament House

The Separation of Queensland from New South Wales in 1859 meant a Parliament House was needed for the new colony but the Queensland Government lacked funds to build one. Legend has it that when Queensland's new Treasurer inspected the funds there was only nine pence in hand.

The new capital city lacked a hospital of suitable size for a growing population, a Supreme Court, a Government House and a Parliament House. However, for the first 10 years government funds were insufficient to consider constructing any major buildings. This meant that the Queensland Parliament was forced to continue holding its sessions in the grim surroundings of the former Convict Barracks on Queen Street.

The discovery of gold in the Gympie region improved Queensland's financial position considerably.

In the early 1860s, a competition was held to select the most suitable design for the new Parliament House on a site in George Street. The competition was won by Charles Tiffin, the newly appointed Colonial Architect, who designed the facade in the neoclassical style.

In 1865, the Foundation Stone of Queensland's Parliament House was laid with due pomp and ceremony. John Petrie, son of Andrew Petrie and Brisbane's leading building contractor, carried out the work to the highest standards. Construction work took three years and was completed exactly on schedule early in August 1868, which is rarely the case for a public building.

On 4 August 1868, the first session of Parliament took place in the new Parliament House. Acting Governor Colonel Maurice O'Connell, deputising for Governor Samuel Blackall, opened the first session on behalf of Her Majesty Queen Victoria.

Parliament House adjoined the Botanic Gardens, so Members could take a walk or relax there. The stone building and its interior fittings of hand-polished Canungra cedar cost the public purse £62,435, which at that time was an enormous sum. It paid for superbly decorated suites for the Premier, the Speaker and other important officials of the Parliament, and an Upper House or Legislative Council. Unfortunately, the Legislative Council was abolished in 1922.

Tiffin's original design for Government House had been adapted from northern French rather than Italian architecture and was not really suitable for a building in subtropical Queensland. Following complaints by Members about the stifling heat during the summer, wide verandahs were added to the facade in the summer of 1880. When the American artist William Fitler made his engraving [plate 36] the arches and shaded verandahs had been added. Eleven years later an extension facing Alice Street was added.

A century after Parliament House was built it had become inadequate to house all the facilities needed in the world of changing technology and greater Parliamentary responsibilities. So, in 1979, the Parliamentary Annexe with increased space for offices, committee rooms and information facilities was built alongside Parliament House. By then Charles Tiffin's building had become an important Brisbane landmark, so extensive restoration and augmentation work was undertaken on this important heritage building.

In 1882, the building of the Queensland Parliament was the scene of a bizarre incident when it was nearly fired on by ss *Gayundah*, a gunboat commanded by Captain Henry Wright.

Having been denied the right to take shore leave the captain brought the ship upriver facing Parliament House. Feeling he had been dealt with unfairly, Captain Wright trained the *Gayundah*'s guns on Parliament House and prepared to open fire. The crew were divided into those who supported their captain and those who supported the Queensland Government. Verbal and physical battles raged. Officers and ratings gave each other black eyes and bloody noses and hurled bottles and chairs at each other. Eventually, the Government supporters won the day and Captain Wright was persuaded to abandon his comic opera mutiny.

Plate 36. PARLIAMENT HOUSE, CORNER OF GEORGE AND ALICE STREETS *after* WILLIAM C. FITLER. *Engraved from a watercolour, initialled lower left and reproduced in 1888. Parliament House was designed by Charles Tiffin in neoclassical style with a French influence and an Italianate dome. The building was inaugurated in 1868 but Members complained of the heat in summer so the colonnades shown here were added in 1880.*
The engraving was published in **The Picturesque Atlas of Australasia, 1888.**

Authors' collection.

The Royal Brisbane Hospital

The main building of what was initially named the Bowen Hospital in Herston was designed by the architect Charles Tiffin, although other architects were also involved. A hospital of the proposed size was long overdue. The original Convict Hospital on North Quay was grossly overcrowded as epidemics of diseases brought in from the tropics regularly swept through subtropical Brisbane. Malaria, dengue fever, typhus, typhoid, amoebic dysentery and smallpox were notorious killers of Brisbane's white population. There were also frequent surgical emergencies caused by gunshot wounds and knife injuries resulting from numerous bar-room and street brawls.

In the 1860s tropical diseases were brought to Queensland by the unfortunate South Sea Islanders who were kidnapped and taken aboard the infamous 'blackbirding' ships and brought to Brisbane and northern Queensland where they were forced to work on cotton plantations and cane fields. Although some of them were well treated, others worked under slave labour conditions. Many of them died but not before they had bequeathed diseases to their white employers. Blackbirding became more strictly controlled in the 1870s. Fortunately, the practice was outlawed by the Queensland Government in the 1890s and most Islanders were sent home.

With funds frozen by the Treasury in New South Wales in the period immediately following Separation,

Plate 37.   BOWEN HOSPITAL NEAR BRISBANE [NOW THE ROYAL BRISBANE HOSPITAL] by HENRY GRANT LLOYD.
Pencil and watercolour, signed and dated lower right 9 May 1873.

Mitchell Library, Sydney.

the building of a larger hospital with a separate nurses' home was forced to wait until Queensland accumulated sufficient funds of its own.

Eventually, the new hospital was built under the supervision of Andrew Petrie and completed in 1867. It stood on open land at Herston, surrounded by former convict stone quarries. A large park provided isolation for the Fever Wards; the long, low blocks were located just behind the main building and set amid spacious landscaped grounds. However, some people wrote angry letters to the newspapers, complaining that the new hospital was sited too far out of the town and should have been built at Spring Hill or Petrie Terrace.

The Bowen or Brisbane General Hospital, [later incorporated into today's Royal Brisbane], was responsible for saving countless lives and helped greatly to lower Queensland's previously high death rate. Over 2,000 cases of typhoid were admitted to the wards between 1880 and 1896.

Queensland in its early days had a considerably higher death rate than the rest of Australia. The majority of severe cases of diseases from the tropics were dealt with by this one hospital. Diseases were also caused by the rapid influx of immigrant labour to Brisbane, bound for the Queensland goldfields, including the horrifying outbreak of bubonic plague, which was carried ashore to Brisbane by shipboard rats.

Much valuable and original research was pioneered in the hospital's laboratories and on its wards.

The first Resident Surgeon of the Hospital, Dr Joseph Bancroft, became internationally celebrated for research into the role of insects and parasites in the transmission of tropical diseases. In 1887 Bancroft published his discovery that much of the blindness in the tropics was caused by the adult female filarial worm. His research into tropical diseases made the Brisbane General Hospital famous in medical circles overseas and led to the successful treatment of filariasis.

Bancroft's work assisted in the successful settlement by Europeans of subtropical Brisbane and the tropical north of Queensland at a time when the tropics were seen as 'the white man's grave'. Undulant fever, filariasis and other worm infestations, previously unknown in the Colony, together with the occasional case of leprosy, added to Bowen Hospital's heavy workload.

Today the Royal Brisbane Hospital is one of the largest hospital complexes in the Southern Hemisphere.

Cintra House

Cintra House was designed by architect Benjamin Backhouse and is situated on the slopes of the Bowen Hills. The house was later extended by Richard Gailey.

The fourteen acres of land surrounding Cintra House were originally owned by Brisbane author Nehemiah Bartley, who sold the land to the Webb brothers, wealthy import and export merchants. The Webbs had offices on Eagle Street. They also owned the land on which Cintra House stands but lived there in a much smaller house than the present one.

In 1877, the original house and grounds were sold to businessman and grazier Boyd Morehead, who was a Member of the Queensland Legislative Assembly for Mitchell, where he owned large sheep properties. Morehead, then a very wealthy man, enlarged Cintra House to use it as his Brisbane residence during parliamentary sittings. Morehead was a witty, well-educated and well-travelled man. The house was named 'Cintra' after he and his wife had visited the Portuguese town named Cintra on their honeymoon.

The gardens were landscaped by the Moreheads in the 'Gardenesque Style', which was fashionable for elegant houses of that period in Britain, New South Wales and Victoria.

At the time Rayment painted the watercolour, shown on plate 38, labour was very cheap. Elaborate flower-beds, massed with different coloured annuals, needed frequent attention to keep them at their best. A sweeping gravelled carriage drive and manicured lawns would have needed long hours of work by gardeners.

In Boyd Morehead's time, even such a spacious home as Cintra House became too small for himself, his wife, eight children and all the servants who attended them. To accommodate so many people, he added a children's wing to the south side of the main house.

Years later, he added the bay window at the end of the porch and the fine iron-lace verandahs.

Morehead's Premiership lasted only two years. A highly intelligent man, his ironic wit and aggressive championship of the cause of the squatters made him many enemies. His short Premiership is remembered for establishing an endurance record, when the Assembly sat continuously for 97 hours without a break

After the death of his first wife in 1890, Boyd Morehead remarried and had another child. He died at Cintra House in 1905 and his widow sold the property. From then on, Cintra House had a variety of wealthy owners.

In 1925 the entire Cintra property, including the house itself, was split into two separate homes. The passageway between the main house and Morehead's southern extension was demolished and a dividing fence was built. The southern extension became a private nursing home.

As essential repairs were left undone the main house was allowed to run down. By the early 1970s the garden had become a wreck. The central flowerbed, seen in the painting, and the gravelled drive disappeared and the grass on the lawns was waist-high. By 1973 no one lived in the house and it had become derelict. Vagrants had lit fires in the once elegant drawing room, the walls were covered in graffiti and valuable fittings had been ripped from their sockets and stolen.

Finally, Wayne Kratzmann and his partner, John Weaver, restored the house exquisitely. They turned it into Cintra Galleries, famous for art and antiques, but several years later they moved their business to Cintra Galleries on Park Road, Milton [now the premises of the Mary Ryan Bookshop]. Since then the original Cintra House has changed hands several times.

Plate 38.   CINTRA HOUSE AND GARDENS by ROBERT SAUNDER RAYMENT. Water-colour, signed and dated lower left, 1888. At this time, Cintra's owner, Boyd Morehead was Premier of Queensland.

From a private collection.

The Old Supreme Court

On 11 February 1842, the order proclaiming the Moreton Bay District Penal Settlement out of bounds to free settlers was rescinded by the New South Wales Government. The Moreton Bay district and Brisbane Town were now areas where 'settlers and other free persons' were at liberty to settle.

Brisbane Town was to be surveyed, subdivided and blocks of land offered for sale by the New South Wales Government. The Moreton Bay area was to be under the jurisdiction of the Police Magistrate, Captain John Wickham, a former naval officer who had sailed with Conrad Martens and Charles Darwin aboard *The Beagle*.

Blocks of land along the river in North and South Brisbane and Kangaroo Point were sold by auction or tender in Sydney. Small investors, land speculators, sawmill owners and shopkeepers bought these first blocks as did some wealthy Darling Downs and Brisbane River Valley squatters who wanted a stake in the new town and its surrounding agricultural land.

Captain Wickham's duties included that of magistrate for minor crimes, while all major crimes were tried in Sydney. There was no courtroom available in Brisbane Town so Captain Wickham had to use the old Convict Barracks on Queen Street. On Sundays the courtroom became a place of worship for the first settlers.

As North and South Brisbane were part of New South Wales, the first Supreme Court session held on 15 April 1857 was referred to as the *New South Wales Supreme Court at Moreton Bay,* presided over by Mr Justice Samuel Frederick Milford.

A Supreme Court for Queensland was not established until Separation from New South Wales had taken place.

In 1859 Mr Justice Milford was appointed Queensland's first judge but he returned to Sydney after a short while. On 14 August 1861 his place was taken by Justice Lutwyche, after whom the suburb of Lutwyche was named.

Since there was still no money for a courthouse the Supreme Court had to operate from the grim premises of the former Convict Barracks, which also served as a temporary Parliament House until money could be found to build a proper Parliament House.

It took until 1875 to find enough government money to erect the imposing Supreme Court on the corner of North Quay, Ann and George Streets. The building was designed in the neoclassical style by Francis Drummond Greville Stanley, architect of the Ports and Harbours Building and the Queensland Club, details of whose life can be found in Don Watson and Judith McKay's book, *Queensland Architects of the 19th Century*.

The contract to build the Supreme Court was awarded to the construction firm headed by John Petrie.

The Supreme Court's opening ceremony took place on 6 March 1879 in front of Queensland's legal 'eagles' and parliamentarians. Built on classical lines and with columned verandahs, this handsome building, seen here from the main entrance on North Quay, served as Queensland's Supreme Court for almost a century.

The building was badly damaged by fire in September 1968 and was demolished in 1976. Today there would be a public outcry over demolishing such a handsome stone structure rather than incorporating its facade into a larger development. Finally this historic and very substantial stone building was replaced by brand-new Supreme Court, a functional edifice of concrete and glass, especially designed to cope with the demands of a technological age.

Plate 39.   THE OLD SUPREME COURT BUILDING, NORTH QUAY, c. 1885, after WILLIAM CROTHERS FITLER. The original drawing was specially commissioned from this American artist and published as a wood engraving in **The Picturesque Atlas of Australasia, 1888**. It shows one of Brisbane's finest early buildings, demolished a century later after being seriously damaged by fire.

The Asylum at Woogaroo

In the early days of free settlement, the mentally ill were kept in chains or straightjackets in the overcrowded Convict Hospital on North Quay. Mentally ill patients who were considered a danger to others or themselves were housed in the Female Factory on Queen Street, which served as Brisbane's gaol.

A new asylum was designed by Chief Draftsman Eustace Harries of the Works Department. Work began on the new Woogaroo Asylum in 1862. By January 1865, the first patients were transferred from the gaol to the infamous Woogaroo Asylum 'up river'. It is hard to know which one of these two places was worse.

Before the discovery of psychiatric drugs, restraints for violent patients included forcible immersion in a cold bath, long periods spent blindfolded while roped to a chair or putting the patient in a straitjacket. Within two years ugly rumours of conditions at the Asylum started to circulate. Questions were asked in the Legislative Assembly. An official Government Inquiry was held in 1869, confirming the horrific tales of maltreatment and sexual abuse of patients. Many of the 'nurses' were revealed as former criminals or Ipswich prostitutes. As a result, practically the entire nursing staff was dismissed.

Much later, in an effort to rehabilitate the Asylum's reputation, its name was changed to Wolston Park Hospital, after the birthplace of Dr Stephen Simpson. The doctor had lived in the adjacent residence called Wolston House [now owned by the National Trust].

Dr Simpson, one of the pioineers of medicine in Brisbane, waited for many years before he was in a suitable position to marry the woman he loved and offer her a fine home. Sadly, the doctor's wife died in childbirth. Prostrate with grief he remained living at Wolston House as a virtual recluse.

Dr Simpson aimed to pass on the house and surrounding land to his favourite nephew, named J. M. Ommaney. He invited young Ommaney to sail out from England and stay with him at Wolston House.

Disaster struck again when the doctor's nephew was thrown from his horse and died. This happened in the shadow of the hill Dr Simpson named *Mount Ommaney* in his nephew's memory.

Plate 40.

THE LUNATIC ASYLUM AT WOOGAROO, KNOWN AS WOLSTON PARK HOSPITAL. *Line and wash drawing by Eustace Henry Harries, c. 1865.*

John Oxley Library, Brisbane.

The General Post Office

In convict days, letters were expensive to send to Brisbane. They were entrusted to shipping companies in Britain, which charged a fee for each letter, stamped it as paid and gave the letter to the purser or captain of supply ships which called at Brisbane. When ships arrived at the wharf all letters were delivered to a small building in Queen Street which also served as the married soldiers' quarters. Most letters were for the officers as many soldiers and convicts were illiterate.

In 1840 Rowland Hill established the British Postal Service and special stamps were printed bearing the Queen's image to show that postage had been paid.

After Brisbane was declared open for free settlement more and more people arrived, with the result that the volume of mail grew substantially. In response a design competition was held for a new Post Office.

John Barr won the competition, but after further consideration his design for a monumental building with an imposing clock tower was found to be too costly. But Barr's design was accepted after George Payne had modified it. In 1871, John Petrie's construction company started work in compliance with the modified design.

The General Post Office was built in two stages. The northern wing with its cast-iron balustrades was completed in September 1872. By then the Queensland Government had decided to amalgamate the postal and electrical telegraph services, so the following year the southern wing, designed by F.D.G. Stanley was built to house the new Electric Telegraph Department. Both wings were joined by a central block.

Although numerous alterations and renovations have been carried out over the years, the essential character of Brisbane's handsome General Post Office building has been retained to the present day.

Plate 41.   BRISBANE'S FIRST GENERAL POST OFFICE, circa 1864. The doorway on the right leads to the old solitary cells.
Courtesy John Oxley Library, State Library of Queensland, Brisbane.

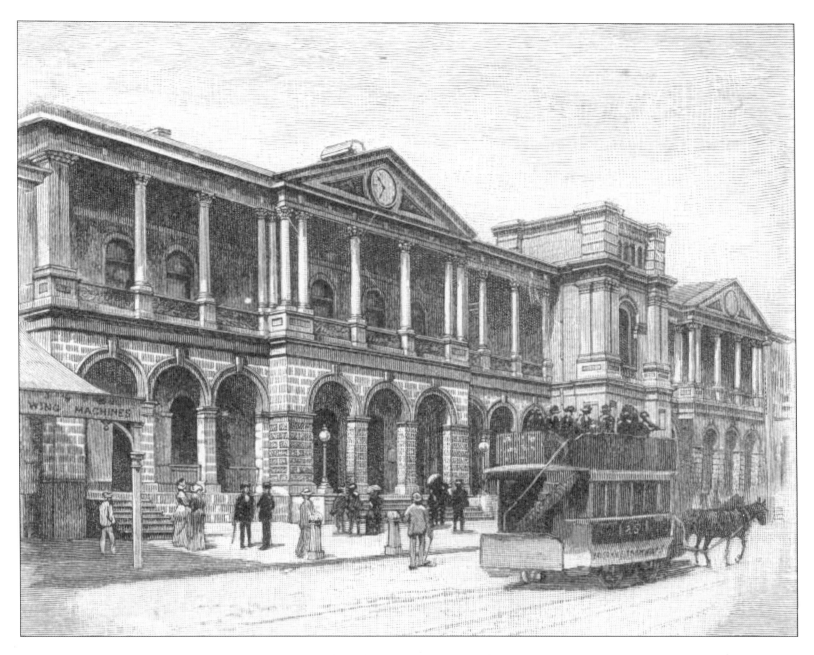

Plate 42. THE NEW GENERAL POST OFFICE. The left [northern] wing was opened on 28 September 1872. In 1879 the right [southern] wing, to house the Electrical Telegraph Department, was completed. A horse-drawn tram in the foreground of the picture demonstrates how the former convict settlement was keeping abreast of the latest developments.
This engraving was published in **The Picturesque Atlas of Australasia, 1888**.

Authors' collection.

Wickham Terrace

Conversion of the Windmill

After 1841, the Windmill was no longer used for grinding maize, probably due to further problems with the sails. In 1849, it was proposed to sell the property for redevelopment, but a public outcry saved one of Brisbane's last convict-built structures.

In 1862, it housed the Natural History Collections of the Queensland Museum. In 1865, the Windmill became a Signal Station and Observatory. By that time, the sails and the domed top had been removed and a flagpole had been erected. A time ball was installed on top of the mill and at precisely one o'clock every afternoon the time ball was dropped. This then served as a signal for a gun to be fired so the citizens of Brisbane could set their clocks to the correct time.

The Observation Galleries can clearly be seen in this detailed engraving. In the 1930s, no longer an observatory, the Windmill was used for some of Brisbane's first experiments in television. It still stands today on Wickham Terrace, where its site has been preserved as a park by the Brisbane City Council.

Plate 43. WICKHAM TERRACE, 1865.
This unsigned drawing was published in 1868 as an engraving by **The Australian Journal**.

'High Society' on the Terrace

By 1865, Wickham Terrace was inhabited by some of the wealthier people in Brisbane. Elegantly dressed ladies in crinolines and bonnets walked their children and their dogs 'on the Terrace' as it was known. Neat paling fences enclosed well-tended gardens. The road to the former convict windmill was still a dirt road, but forgotten were the days when convicts in heavy leg irons shuffled up the steeply sloping track to work for long hours on the treadmill.

The stone house in the centre of the engraving [plate 43] was designed by Benjamin Backhouse, the architect son of a stonemason. The house was named *Alexandra* after the wife of the original owner. After it was demolished and replaced by a block of medical and professional rooms the name *Alexandra* was retained for the new building. Handsome private residences on the Terrace housed some of Brisbane's leading families, whose wives and children were driven to the Queen Street shops in horse-drawn carriages handled by liveried coachmen.

An observant journalist on the staff of the *Queensland Daily Guardian* wrote in November 1863:

> Along Wickham Terrace there is a row of handsome villa residences, occupied chiefly by the leading businessmen of the town. When their day's work is done, they go by a steep ascent from their money-grubbing counting houses to their comfortable homes on the Terrace.

Around 1885 Frederick Schell painted Wickham Terrace with the old Windmill as its focal point [plate 44]. Schell's view of 'The Terrace' shows it during the years of Brisbane's unparalleled financial boom, when revenues from mines like Mount Morgan and huge pastoral fortunes from the Downs paid for the latest Paris fashions to be worn at Brisbane's Opera House.

The picture shows one of Brisbane's earliest telephone lines, which connected what was now the Observatory to the City Fire Station since the beginning of the 1880s. Some of the residents of elite Wickham Terrace gladly paid the huge sums that it cost to obtain the luxury of a 'speaking' apparatus.

The Terrace retained its social superiority until the invention of motorised transport, which meant that the elite could move farther away from the City. Many of Brisbane's wealthy gradually moved to areas such as Coorparoo, Ascot, Hamilton and Indooroopilly.

The era of Queensland's prosperity ended abruptly with the financial crash of 1893, which devastated so many self-made men.

The expanding medical profession finally took over the old mansions on the Terrace for their consulting rooms. Today blocks of professional rooms still carry the names of the original residents of the 1850s, such as Ballow Chambers, named after Dr David Ballow, one of Brisbane's earliest Government Medical Officers.

Plate 44. WICKHAM TERRACE c. 1885 after FREDERICK B. SCHELL. Engraving from a pencil and wash drawing.

From the collection of Derek and Kathryn Nicholls.

North and South Brisbane, 1850–60

In 1855, Thomas Baines paid a brief visit to Brisbane and made a pencil sketch called *South Brisbane from North Brisbane* [National Library]. Baines was the artist on Sir Augustus Gregory's expedition to North Australia. He was also the expedition's storeman.

The artist depicted Brisbane as a rough frontier town of timber cottages with shingled roofs. Thirteen years after making his pencil sketch Baines made a finished oil painting from it [plate 46], destined for an exhibition in London to increase immigration to Queensland.

It is a mystery why J.C. Armytage, a minor British artist who never visited Brisbane in his life, copied Baines' foreground in his engraving *North Brisbane from South Brisbane*. The engraving was published in Edwin Carton Booth's book *Australia Illustrated with Drawings*, published in two parts in 1874–76.

The two views are from opposite sides of the Brisbane River, but an almost identical scene appears in the foreground of both works [compare plate 45 with plate 46]. They show the same timber cottages with banana trees, maize plants and pineapples growing in their back gardens. The picket fences and the covered wagon, traversing a dirt track, are also identical.

Armytage's view on this page seems to be partly taken from photographs, probably by Richard Daintree, while the oil by Thomas Baines may have been drawn from life.

Baines titled his painting *South Brisbane from the North Shore* [of the Brisbane River]. Aiming to produce a dramatic image Baines showed naked Aborigines brandishing spears. Armytage was making his drawing for a book on Australia that aimed to persuade the British to emigrate there and for that reason he may have been told to remove the spears.

Baines shows sailing ships obscuring the A.S.N. Company's Wharf on Stanley Quay, future site of the South Bank Cultural complex. It is the same wharf that appears in the view by Captain Owen Stanley [plate 29].

Armytage shows the developing town of North Brisbane, including the triangular pediment of the convict-built Government Store on William Street, doubtless engraved from photographs.

The fact that an engraving by Armytage, a man who never visited Australia, could be used in a popular book shows what a shortage there was of visual material on this frontier town. In the 1860s and 1870s, Brisbane had few professional artists and lacked an art gallery, unlike Sydney, which had a plethora of artists to depict the city.

Plate 45. NORTH BRISBANE FROM SOUTH BRISBANE. Engraving by J. C. Armytage, printed in England c. 1876.

Private collection.

Plate 46.   SOUTH BRISBANE FROM THE NORTH SHORE [of the Brisbane River], 1868. Oil painting by Thomas Baines [1820-1875], based on a pencil sketch by the same artist. The painting was probably exhibited in London that year when the foreground was copied by J.C. Armytage for an engraving to be included in Edwin Carton Booth's book on Australia.[plate 45].

National Library of Australia, Canberra.

Plate 47a. *A recent photograph taken from the corner of Alice and William Streets, showing the Riverside Freeway and South Bank across the Brisbane River with Mount Coot-tha to the rear. Both Owen Stanley [plate 29] and Thomas Baines [plate 46] made their views from approximately the same spot. Dominant buildings in the picture are the Rydges hotel, the Convention Centre and the Queensland Performing Arts Centre.*

© *Pandanus Press.*

Plate 47b. A recent photograph taken from Grey Street, South Brisbane, showing the city across the Brisbane River. Brisbane has come a long way since J.C. Armytage showed this view in his engraving of 1876, taken from approximately the same spot [plate 45].

© *Pandanus Press.*

Plate 48.   BRISBANE WHARVES FROM BOWEN TERRACE. *Unsigned watercolour by an unknown artist.*
Courtesy Tim McCormick, Rare Books, Sydney.

Plate 49.   BULIMBA REACH, BREAKFAST CREEK BRIDGE AND BOWEN HILLS FROM TOORAK HOUSE, HAMILTON. *Pen and wash drawing by Lady Eliza Hodgson, bearing the inscription lower left 'BRISBANE FROM TOORAK, JULY 1869.*
Mitchell Library, Sydney.

Brisbane Views of the 1860s

Brisbane Wharves

Although painted years earlier by an unknown artist, the watercolour depicted on plate 48 can be compared with the oil painting *Panorama of Brisbane from Bowen Terrace in 1880*, executed by Joseph Augustus Clarke [plate 63]. Both works portray the busy, sprawling settlement, which had gradually developed along the Brisbane River and identify the major landmarks. The accurate details of buildings and streetscape make it one of the finest topographical paintings of early Brisbane.

The promontory depicted on the left is Kangaroo Point. When sketched by Conrad Martens in 1851, Kangaroo Point was considered one of Brisbane's choicest residential areas. The addition of sawmills and engineering works changed its character entirely. Another feature shown here is the small cable ferry, which plied between Kangaroo Point and North Brisbane.

Public buildings on the far side of the river include Queensland's handsome Parliament House, which can just be seen in the distance. This building took seven years to erect and upon completion in 1868 was regarded as the city's finest structure. Government House and the Botanic Gardens are located further to the left. To the right of Parliament House are Adelaide Street, Wickham Terrace, the John Petrie Office Building and the Gas Works as well as the Municipal Wharves.

In the foreground the painting depicts houses and gardens with lush tropical vegetation; these give some indication of the lifestyle enjoyed by wealthier residents.

Queensland underwent a population explosion during the late 1860s. Thousands of immigrants from overseas and from New South Wales arrived in Queensland, many intending to join the search for gold, and this influx contributed to the expansion of the city.

Hamilton and Bowen Hills

Eliza Hodgson, pupil of Conrad Martens and Brisbane's first trained female artist, painted *Bulimba Reach from Hamilton* from the grounds of Toorak House where she was a house guest of the Dickson family. Like many of Brisbane's most prestigious homes, Toorak House was built on a hilltop to catch the breezes. Lady Hodgson presented her finished watercolour to her Brisbane hosts, Sir James and Lady Annie Dickson. Sir James Dickson and Sir Arthur Hodgson were both members of the Queensland Government. Sir James Dickson would become Premier of Queensland while Sir Arthur Hodgson was Colonial Secretary.

Toorak House has passed through many different hands. It gave its name to Toorak Road while neighbouring Annie and Dickson Streets commemorate Lady Annie Dickson.

The watercolour [plate 49] shows the Bulimba Reach from Hamilton, looking south-west across the mouth of Breakfast Creek to Bowen Hills. The wealthy built on the crests of the hills around Brisbane. In contrast, the cottages of Brisbane artisans were down in valleys, which often flooded and received less cooling breezes.

Although hardly distinguishable in the painting, large houses were built on the crowns of hills, such as Cintra House, owned by wealthy Eagle Street merchant George D. Webb [who sold it to pastoralist and politician Boyd Morehead] and Montpelier, home of architect and businessman James Cowlishaw, who designed many of Brisbane's important commercial edifices. Montpelier would eventually be demolished to erect Cloudland Ballroom, which was Brisbane's wartime entertainment area. Newstead House is just visible in the painting.

The Building Boom of the 1880s

Brisbane Boys Grammar School

Under the *Grammar Schools Act of 1860*, to obtain government endowments to build a private school it was necessary to match the sum requested from the Queensland Government by private subscriptions.

The first grammar school was established at Ipswich and then the rapidly expanding town of Brisbane took only three years to find the necessary money, so eager were the wealthier families to found a good school for the education of their children.

On 29 February 1868, H.R.H. Prince Alfred, Duke of Edinburgh, attended a special ceremony to lay the foundation stone of the Brisbane Grammar School. The school opened a year later and was built in what was then a very tranquil area around Roma Street. This ceremony was one of the most select gatherings in Brisbane. It gave the new school prestige throughout Queensland and northern New South Wales.

Unfortunately, by the mid-1870s, the Grammar School found itself virtually next door to the rapidly expanding railway yards of Roma Street. The noise, grime and the smoke were unpleasant. During the building boom of the 1880s, when loans were freely available, a new site on Gregory Terrace with possibilities for expansion was selected, since the school now had a long waiting list.

The new Brisbane Boys Grammar School was completed in the early 1880s, under the supervision of the architect James Cowlishaw, a resident of Bowen Hills. Subsequent additions, including the Great Hall, a small hospital, a boarding house and house master's residence were designed by the architect Richard Gailey and built between 1883 and 1886.

Brisbane Boys Grammar School boasted Australia's most famous 19th-century principal, Reginald Heber Roe, who had been educated at Balliol College, Oxford. He was a rare combination of a brilliant scholar and athlete. During his 33 years' leadership, he adopted a then-revolutionary attitude for the encouragement of sport and physical fitness as part of the school curriculum while still maintaining exceptionally high educational standards.

In 1893 the *Picturesque Atlas of Australasia* described the Grammar School in the following words,

> A handsome brick edifice in the Gothic style, consisting of a main building with two cross buildings at its ends and a large hall across the centre. This hall is fitted with two large stained-glass windows, one of which contains pictures of Queen Victoria. The grounds are attractively planted with English and tropical flowers and trees; and the two Moreton Bay figs, planted by the two Princes are especially handsome and thrive vigorously.

Princes H.R.H. Prince Albert Victor and H.R.H. Prince George Edward [crowned as King George V] were sons of the future Edward VII. The diary kept by the young Prince of his Australian visit would later be published as a book, entitled *The Cruise of the H.M.S. Bacchant*.

The diary contains the Prince's entry:

> Aug. 19th 1881. Breakfast at Government House: we set off soon afterwards, a party of twenty or thirty of us in all, some on horseback, others in buggies… we all went up to the Brisbane Grammar.

Brisbane Girls Grammar School

A demand for better educational facilities for girls led to a commission for Richard Gailey to design a female equivalent to Brisbane Boys Grammar School on Gregory Terrace. Work on a handsome building incorporating arched verandahs took place between 1882 and 1886.

As more funds were raised, Gailey was instructed to add additions to the school such as staff accommodation and a gymnasium. A library and other additions were added throughout the 1890s and helped to prevent Gailey going bankrupt in this lean period as the Girls Grammar School prospered and grew apace.

Plate 50 [above].
BRISBANE BOYS GRAMMAR SCHOOL ON GREGORY TERRACE, 1881. Unsigned engraving showing the recently completed building, just after the school had moved from Roma Street.

Private collection.

Plate 51 [left].
BRISBANE GIRLS GRAMMAR SCHOOL ON GREGORY TERRACE..

Photograph c. 1930, from a private collection.

The Queensland Club

The Queensland Club in Brisbane was destined to be a place where affluent graziers and professional men could meet. It was Queensland's answer to the lure of traditional London clubs and the Melbourne Club.

In June 1859 Queen Victoria signed Letters Patent creating a brand-new colony which, at her request, was named Queensland, rather than Cooksland as Dr Dunmore Lang and his Scottish supporters had hoped.

Initially, squatters from the Darling Downs and the Brisbane River Valley preferred Ipswich as the capital of the new State of Queensland and *not* Brisbane. Prior to the building of a railway in the 1860s Ipswich had been their gathering place as this was the main outlet for shipping wool from the Darling Downs by barge or river steamer.

To promote Ipswich as Queensland's capital, public meetings were held. However, it soon became evident that the squatters were not going to win their battle. Sleepy little Brisbane Town, divided in two by the Brisbane River, would become Queensland's capital.

The Queensland squatters, aware that their future prospects were bound up with those of the new Government of Queensland, purchased a small brick house in Brisbane's Mary Street. They intended this building to serve as the premises of a new residential club. Many of them hoped to become members of the new Legislative Assembly and wanted somewhere to stay within walking distance of Parliament House. And indeed, several of them succeeded in being elected to the new Queensland Parliament in Brisbane.

On 6 December 1859, four days before Governor Bowen was due to arrive in Brisbane for the inauguration ceremonies of the colony, the Queensland Club opened its doors.

Twenty-three years later, wealthy and powerful club members from various spheres of life decided to commission the local architect Francis Drummond Greville Stanley, a recent member of the club, to design them a much larger premises.

Stanley designed a building in the neoclassical style, which would occupy a site on the corner of Alice and George Street, close to Parliament House.

Construction work began in 1883 and was completed the following year. Club members paid £14,150 and what resulted was one of Australia's finest neoclassical buildings with a handsome stairway and wide cool verandahs. Inside, the reception rooms were furnished with deep leather-covered Chesterfield sofas, baize-topped card tables and paintings. A good library and billiard room were supplied with copies of Australian and British newspapers. The club was intended an all-male sanctum where men could escape from their wives and children. The policy was that 'accompanied ladies may view the ground floor on special occasions'.

The Queensland Club is still decorated with some of the original furniture; a pride in its traditions prevails among the members.

Perhaps the enormous stuffed 'alligator' [more likely a crocodile], shot by a Proserpine member named Bode in the 19th century, which stands on a long table under the main stairs, is thought to provide a deterrent to unsuitable behaviour on the part of visitors! A sighting of this stuffed creature and its fearsome teeth is a memorable experience.

Under successive Country Party governments the Queensland Club became an influential corridor of power. Governors dined here with members from the Legislative Assembly and moguls of the beef, wool and sugar industries.

In the modern world the Queensland Club stands for tradition. Its interiors have been redecorated with good taste and elegance and the cuisine is excellent.

The Bellevue Hotel [which stood opposite the Queensland Club] and several of Brisbane's colonial mansions, as shown in Cranston's drawing of North Quay [plate 89], have been demolished to build towers of concrete, steel and plate glass. However, the Queensland Club remains an oasis of civilised tranquillity and comfort for its members in the midst of a bustling city.

Plate 52.   THE QUEENSLAND CLUB, GEORGE AND ALICE STREETS c. 1885 after WILLIAM C. FITLER'S WATERCOLOUR. *Engraving from the original watercolour, initialled lower left and published in 1886. It shows one of the fine buildings of Brisbane's golden age of architecture, which had just been completed when the American artist William Fitler visited Brisbane. The engraving was published in* **The Picturesque Atlas of Australasia, 1888**.

Authors' collection.

The Treasury Building

Excavations of the site of the former convict Officers' Quarters and Military Barracks, to build a palatial Treasury Building for the Queensland Government, started in 1885, during the building boom.

Construction work was carried out in three stages, starting with the William Street section, which was occupied in 1889. The Elizabeth Street frontage was erected between in 1890 and 1893.

Further extensions were not carried out until after World War l. The George and Queen Street facades were finally completed in 1928.

The lower part of the Treasury Building was built of Brisbane tuff and the facades of the four floors above were built of Queensland sandstone quarried at Helidon, Highfield and Lockyer.

On 12 October 1880 *The Queenslander* reported that

> Before entering upon erection of the Treasury Buildings, the Queensland Government, anxious to get as perfect a design as possible, offers prizes for the three best designs.

A large number of architects residing in various colonies submitted plans for the proposed building.

The colonial architect John James Clark [1838–1915], whose largest work up to then was the Yungaba Immigration Depot, was selected for the design of one of the largest public buildings in Australia. The Liverpool-trained architect designed the building in the Classical Revival style, with facades having an eclectic mix of Ionic, Doric and Corinthian columns. Wide Italian Renaissance-style colonnades were included to protect the interior from direct sunlight and rain. According to J. J. Clarke's design, the building would occupy an entire city block.

When the first stage of the imposing Treasury Building was completed everyone was delighted with the result. The building has a basement, a ground floor with very high ceilings and two upper storeys.

Clarke, a talented but vain man, was eventually lured away to work in Melbourne, where he died.

More than 40 years after its completion the exterior of the building needed cleaning and restoration had to be carried out. Restoration work included the replacement of marble steps to the main Queen Street entrance and extensive repairs to the stonework and re-pointing.

The Treasury Building stood empty for some time after government staff was moved from there to the new Executive Building and other government buildings.

The building was then converted into a casino in the mid-1990s. A conservation report, prepared for the then Government by the local historian Helen Gregory and by Ray Whitmore, former professor of engineering at the University of Queensland, contained recommendations for alternative and more sympathetic uses of the building.

The decision to use such a fine example of period architecture as a casino has been the subject of considerable public disquiet.

Fortunately, the conversion to a casino has left Clarke's fine facade as imposing as the architect intended. The building continues to look very handsome indeed, particularly when floodlit at night.

However, inside the building disquiet has been aroused as the interior has been fitted with the kind of luridly coloured carpets beloved of cinema complexes. These are scarcely in keeping with the dignity of the building.

There are serious concerns about using the Treasury Building as a casino, particularly in view of the universal rise in gambling addiction. Church groups and Gamblers Anonymous, who deal with the casualties of gambling, are not at all happy about its present use.

However, the positive aspect is that conversion of this magnificent building into a casino has ensured that Clarke's creation has been saved from becoming a ruin.

All those who favoured turning the building into a casino, to make money for the Queensland Government, point out that one of Brisbane's most imposing buildings has been saved for posterity without the Government having to spend a fortune on its restoration.

Plate 53 [above].
THE TREASURY BUILDING.
c 1926 — Construction work of the final stage [George and Queen Street wings] has just commenced.

*Plate 54 [left].
A recent photograph of*
THE TREASURY BUILDING, *now used as a casino.*

© *Pandanus Press.*

The Bellevue Hotel

The historic Bellevue Hotel faced Parliament House on one side and the Queensland Club on the other. The upper windows over Alice Street commanded magnificent views of the Botanic Gardens.

The hotel took its name from a small private school called Belle Vue [beautiful view], run by a Miss Lester, which occupied the site from 1859 for a few years. When the school closed, Charles Hanson built a modest private hotel on the site and named it after the school. Hanson's Bellevue Hotel, only one minute's walk away from the Assembly Hall of Parliament House, proved so convenient for country members that it prospered, thanks to their patronage.

However, by the boom years of the 1880s, the hotel's influential and wealthy clientele required more luxurious accommodation. And so the old Bellevue Hotel was bought by J.A. Zahel, an entrepreneurial figure. Zahel, confident of Brisbane's future prospects, invested a large sum of money in a new and more luxurious building to replace the former modest one. No expense was spared to make the Bellevue as attractive and comfortable as possible to attract the custom of the members to its saloons and dining rooms. Additional amenities were incorporated for the Members' families, as well as for the wealthy graziers and their wives who visited Brisbane.

The *Queensland Figaro*, of 12 March 1887, records that the new hotel was

> fitted with a ladies' drawing room, private suites for informal dining, baths with hot and cold water, smoking, writing and reading rooms; a barber attends every morning for the convenience of guests and a waiter meets each steamer on its arrival.

What the newspaper did *not* say was that the 'suites for private dining' contained beds, which some Queensland politicians found ideal for entertaining lady friends.

The Bellevue was the epitome of luxury in a state that was living on credit. Eventually, Mr Zahel ran into financial difficulties and the Bellevue Hotel subsequently changed hands several times.

Set among huge fig trees and flowering jacarandas, the Bellevue retained its unique position in the heart of the city for well over 80 years. Its delicate iron-lace balustrades, spacious verandas and traditional Queensland iron roofs, 'curving down as plumply as a nineties belle' were the subject of an article in the *Sydney Bulletin* around 1900, when it was regarded as *the* prestige hotel of Brisbane.

John Lennon's Hotel on George Street opened in 1884 with 62 bedrooms and attracted distinguished visitors like Dame Nellie Melba. Lennon's Hotel, while pleasant enough, did not have that very special place in the hearts of Queenslanders that the Bellevue enjoyed. Nevertheless, it became *the* place to stay.

After 80 years the Bellevue started to run down. Rumours circulated that the National Party Government of Queensland was planning to redevelop the Bellevue's valuable site and had decided to demolish the historic building. In June 1974, as a preliminary step, the Queensland Government declared the balconies of the Bellevue dangerous to the public and ordered them to be removed, including the beautiful iron lace balustrades. At one fell stroke they eliminated much of the visual appeal of the building [plate 56].

Some members of the National Trust of Queensland still insisted that the Bellevue was a heritage building and had to be saved, but others felt that it was beyond restoration. Many Brisbane residents were outraged when the Coalition Government, in the middle of the fateful night of Saturday 21 April 1979, sent in the bulldozers of a demolition company to destroy the Bellevue.

In Tom Shapcott's book *Hotel Bellevue* and according to reports in the local papers, National Party henchmen engaged demolition contractors who allegedly employed derelicts who were housed under terrible conditions in a camp at Gumdale. Hugh Lunn, author of the Brisbane-based best-seller *Over the Top with Jim,* made the launch of Shapcott's book an unforgettable event. Lunn produced the demolition contractors' advertisement from the *Yellow Pages Directory* and set fire to it amid loud cheers by a Brisbane audience.

The Bellevue's site became part of the land on which a concrete and glass edifice was built.

Plate 55 [above].
THE BELLEVUE HOTEL.
Unsigned pencil drawing published as a wood engraving in 1887.
*The **Bellevue** was renowned for its superb iron lace balustrades.*

Private collection.

Plate 56 [left].
THE BELLEVUE HOTEL.
Photographed after the balustrades had been removed and shortly before the building was demolished.

Private collection.

The Former Queensland Museum

The former Queensland Museum at Bowen Bridge Road was originally built as an exhibition building for the National Agricultural and Industrial Association of Queensland, the organisation who ran the Brisbane 'Ekka'. However, the Agricultural Association lacked capital, had to borrow the money for the exhibition building's construction and ran into debt.

The building was designed by the talented Welsh-born architect George Henry Addison, [1857–1922]. A full description of Addison's career can be found in Donald Watson and Judith McKay's informative book *Queensland Architects of the 19th Century*.

A minister's son, orphaned at the age of 10, Addison was educated on a scholarship and showed great talent in drawing and design. Originally, Addison migrated to Melbourne, where he was befriended by the English-born artist Tom Roberts. Later he came to Brisbane, where he made his mark as an architect and designed Fernbrook, a handsome family home in Indooroopilly. He was bankrupted in the depression of the 1890s but later set up an architect's office again and prospered.

George Addison took his inspiration for the museum, The Mansions and several other buildings from Venetian Gothic architecture, a style influenced by Byzantium, as Venetian and Byzantine history and architecture were closely entwined. Consequently, Addison's old museum is an eclectic mix of Byzantine and Venetian Gothic styles. The side elevation has a row of pointed arches, for which Addison must have been inspired by the arches on the facade of the Doge's Palace in Venice.

The front facade is a fantasy of pinnacles and domed turrets created in rose and cream bricks and cream limestone. Inside, the building had floor-to-ceiling stained glass windows, also designed by Addison. No expense was spared on its construction in the booming 1880s when huge loans were received for building work. Naturally, costs soared as Addison intended to create a masterpiece and employed only the finest materials.

Unfortunately, the building was completed just as the boom faded and turned into an economic depression. During the economic downturn the National Agricultural and Industrial Association was unable to repay the money it had borrowed, so the building had to be taken over by the Queensland Government. Addison's building was too magnificent to leave it untenanted, so on 23 April 1891 it became a combination of a concert hall and home of the Queensland Museum.

At long last Queensland's important geological collections could be put on view. For too long these collections had been poorly housed; first in an upper room in the Post Office and then in the old library on the corner of William Street, the future site of the old State Library of Queensland.

The first chairman of the Board of Trustees of the Museum was none other than the well-known explorer and scientist Sir Augustus Gregory, a resident of Indooroopilly. The most famous curator of the old Queensland Museum was the celebrated botanist Frederick Manson Bailey, whose term of office lasted from 1882 to 1905.

From 1930 to 1974 part of the red-brick Museum building was occupied by the fledgling Queensland Art Gallery before the Gallery and the Museum moved to their present imposing Queensland Cultural Centre at South Bank, designed by another talented Brisbane architect, Robin Gibson.

Many people were fascinated by the former museum's display of a 120 cm iron *bêche-de-mer* or sea cucumber boiling-down tank, commemorating a heroic Queenslander, named Mary Watson, who helped her husband run a *bêche-de-mer* plant on Lizard Island.

On 30 September 1881, one of Mary's Chinese workers was speared to death by Aborigines from the mainland while Mary's husband was away fishing. Desperation lending her strength, Mary climbed into the tank with her baby, attempting in vain to steer it with a paddle. Unfortunately it did not rain for almost a week and Mary and her baby died an agonising death from thirst and exposure. The sight of this tank inspired Susanna de Vries to write *Strength of Spirit* describing Mary's epic voyage in the iron tank.

Today Addison's red-brick Museum building has a new and exciting role as the headquarters of the Queensland Youth Orchestra and other organisations.

Plate 57 [above].
THE FORMER QUEENSLAND MUSEUM ON GREGORY TCE. An engraving based on the original presentation drawing by the architect George Addison.

Private collection.

Plate 58. [left]
A recent photograph of the former Queensland Museum.

© *Pandanus Press.*

The Mansions

At the height of the 1880s boom the Hon. William Patterson and Boyd Morehead contracted Addison and his partners to design The Mansions. George Addison had also designed the former Queensland Museum at Bowen Bridge Road. Addison's interests and skills were wide-ranging. In addition to architectural work, he specialised in the design of Art Nouveau stained glass. He was also the future President of the Queensland Institute of Architects.

The imposing complex of three-storey terrace houses fronting George and Margaret Streets was completed in 1889. Addison had chosen Renaissance rose-red bricks and cream-coloured New Zealand limestone to highlight an eclectic blend of styles. Cast-iron railings were used in front of the building to provide privacy. Stone columns support arched colonnades to shield the interior from the sun. The light and shade from the colonnades give a sense of unity to the twin facades.

The Mansions reflects Addison's skill as its designer, particularly in the repeated application of the Renaissance archways and the pediments over the entrances to each apartment.

Each dwelling had a name chosen by the occupants, such as Chatsworth, The Grange, Lonsdale and Binna Burra. Addison's sense of humour is shown in his placing of two stone cats gazing down on passers-by from the parapets of The Mansions.

The Mansions were renovated as part of the State Government's Precinct Development Scheme. Today they house a variety of shops and a restaurant.

Plate 59.   *THE MANSIONS. A recent photograph, showing the dominant architectural feature of the Renaissance archways and the pediments over the entrances to each apartment.*

© *Pandanus Press.*

Panorama of Brisbane, 1880

Professional landscape artist Joseph Clarke migrated to Brisbane via India in 1870, the reason for leaving Britain being given as 'a weak chest'. Clarke found few patrons for his art, so he worked as a freelance magazine illustrator and etcher from a rented house in Vulture Street. Later he moved to a larger house in Hope Street and after the 1887 flood damaged his home he moved to Norfolk Cottage, Range View Road, South Brisbane.

At that time etching was widely used in magazine and newspaper publishing, so Clarke was employed to illustrate articles for *The Queenslander* and *The Queensland Figaro*. From 1881, he was appointed drawing teacher at the Brisbane School of Arts, which later became part of the Technical College. In 1887, he was appointed Drawing Master to pupils of the Brisbane Girls Grammar School.

Clarke's masterpiece is a 3.6 m long panorama owned by the Queensland Museum but loaned to the Premier's Suite in the Executive Building in George Street [plates 60 and 63]. The panorama, viewed from Bowen Terrace, depicts the wharf, warehouses and office area looking across Kangaroo Point to North Brisbane with the site of today's Admiralty Towers near the centre.

From this panorama we learn a great deal about Brisbane's boom time of the 1880s. The area of the town around Parliament House is seen in the distance. The more industrial area of Kangaroo Point, with the sawmill founded there in 1857 by the brothers Robert and Walter Birley, is shown in the foreground. The sawmill was built on the site of the disused boiling down works of 'Tinker' Campbell. Birley's Sawmill was destroyed by fire in 1869 but rebuilt much closer to the river so that the logs, rafted downriver, could be more easily hauled into the sawmill. Clarke shows logs stacked against each other to dry out.

In 1893, Birley's Sawmill was swept away in the flood, along with many of the steeply gabled weatherboard cottages built by the artisans and farm labourers who lived at Kangaroo Point.

Today the approaches to the Story Bridge cover up what little remained of Birley's Sawmill.

To the rear of the sawmill, Clarke shows the smoking chimney of J.W. Sutton's Iron Foundry. J.W. Sutton also built steamships, steel barges and railway bridges on a site further to the south on Kangaroo Point, well outside the range of Clarke's panoramic view. Eventually Sutton's ship building activities fell on hard times and the site was taken over by Evans Deakin Shipyards. These in their turn were replaced by the Dockside development of luxury apartments and townhouses during the 1980s and 1990s building boom.

Clarke's panorama also depicts the wealthier area of North Brisbane and shows the solidly built stone home of Dr Hobbs. The doctor had arrived in Brisbane as the ship's surgeon on the *Chaseley*, Dr Lang's migrant ship. In the mid-1850s he built himself an exceptionally fine stone home on Adelaide Street, which was considered 'the best house in Brisbane Town'.

Dr Hobbs lost most of his garden by mistake. Legend relates that the unfortunate doctor returned from an overseas visit to find that a large area of his garden had vanished. Without the doctor's knowledge the area had been excavated by Council workmen to make a smoother continuation of Adelaide Street into Queen Street. Dr Hobbs hired a lawyer and sought compensation, but it was revealed that the destroyed part of his garden had actually encroached onto Council land.

When Queensland separated from New South Wales in 1859, Dr Hobbs agreed to rent his home to the cash-strapped Queensland Government for the sum of £350 a year so the first Governor of Queensland, Sir George Ferguson Bowen, and his wife Lady Diamantina, could live in the doctor's house. At the time there were insufficient funds available to build a proper Government House.

From the upper verandah of Dr Hobbs' rented house, Sir George Ferguson Bowen was sworn into office by Mr Justice Lutwyche in front of a crowd of thousands who had assembled along Adelaide Street and upriver.

The doctor's home would later become the Deanery of St John's Cathedral.

Plate 60. PANORAMA OF BRISBANE FROM BOWEN TERRACE IN 1880 by JOSEPH AUGUSTUS CLARKE [see also colour plate 63]. This magnificent oil measuring 120 x 360 cm has been reproduced by kind permission of the Queensland Museum and the Queensland State Government. It currently hangs in the Executive Building and highlights the considerable expansion of the city which took place in the 1870s, due to high immigration and increasing prosperity from exports of wool, beef, sugar, cotton and gold.

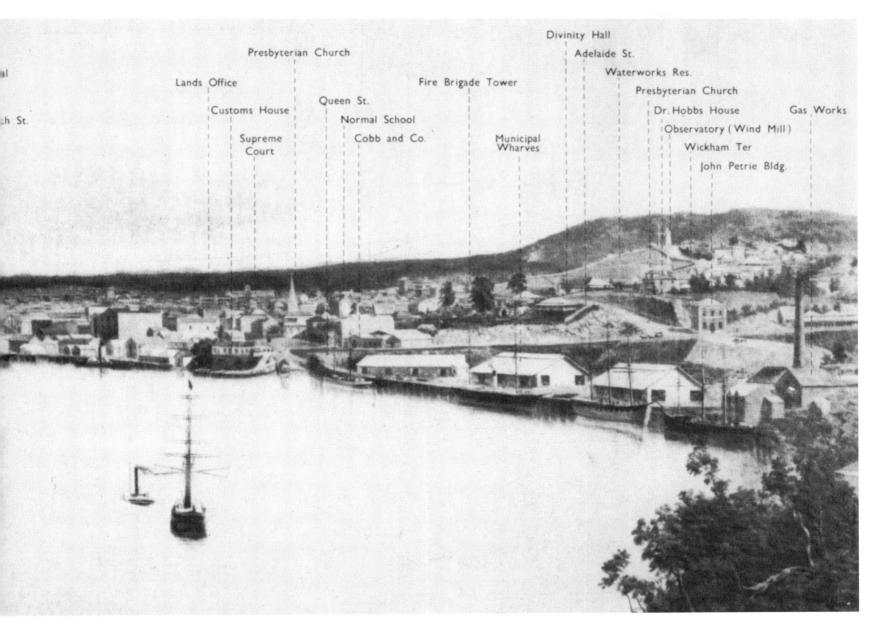

The streets of Brisbane stretched up to Wickham Terrace; the Adelaide Street extension to Queen Street had just been completed. The Edward Street and Customs House ferries ran regularly between the city and the Kangaroo Point Sawmill and Engineering Works, which offered employment to many local residents. On this black and white reproduction of the painting major buildings, streets and other features have been marked.

Windermere

The design of Windermere, 14 Sutherland Avenue, Ascot, has been attributed to architect Benjamin Backhouse [1829–1904]. The corner pavilion or gazebo suggests the involvement of the younger architect Irish-born Richard Gailey [1834–1924], who also worked on Moorlands .

The distinctive corner pavilion with shutters that can be opened to catch the breezes is balanced by a large bay on the far side of this handsome home. The attractive black and white blinds are a modern addition. The house, designed for a sub-tropical climate, was named after an English lake and was constructed on part of the estate of James Sutherland. In her notable book on Queensland architecture Janet Hogan describes Windermere, with its wide verandahs, as an important example of Queensland's colonial architecture.

This significant house with its library and wine cellar was built in the late 1880s for John Sutherland's daughter, Ruth, who married John George Appel, a solicitor and pastoralist of German descent. Photographs show the Appel children in sailor suits, enjoying tennis parties and tea on the verandah and reveal the pleasant leisurely lifestyle of wealthy Ascot and Hamilton residents. Born in South Brisbane, John George rose to prominence as member of the Legislative Assembly and Home Secretary.

Windermere was bought by Charles Frederick White in 1918, was later owned by George Kermode Jeffrey and then by Dr Ellis Murphy and his wife Mary. In 1928 Dr Murphy became Professor of Medicine. The house was later renovated and re-decorated by Mr and Mrs Bentley, formerly of Chelmer, and then sold again.

Moorlands

Moorlands was built in 1892–93 for Mrs Mary Mayne, widow of butcher-turned-property developer Patrick Mayne. On his deathbed Patrick allegedly confessed to the murder of Robert Cox, for which another man had been hung.

The Mayne family bought large acreages of land above Coronation Drive. They commissioned Richard Gailey to design a gabled house with stuccoed walls, bay windows and iron-lace verandahs, with a unique viewing tower or belvedere. Moorlands was surrounded by acres of landscaped grounds and a high fence.

Four of Patrick and Mary Mayne's children lived there, including Patrick's son, the Brisbane lawyer Isaac Mayne, who allegedly murdered Tatsuzo Tobita but who was never charged with his murder. Some physicians think that Isaac may have suffered from porphyria, a hereditary disease leading to madness, or he may have suffered from syphilis. Isaac's brother, Dr James Mayne kept his mad, murderous brother locked away and had the window of Isaac's room boarded up.

Rumours of murder and inherited madness among the Maynes abounded. As a result, Dr James Mayne and his sister, Mary Emilia [who was of very limited intellectual capacity and was never allowed out by herself], were shunned by Brisbane's 'polite society'. Fearing hereditary illness, neither of them married. Kindly Dr James Mayne channelled his energies and capabilities into schemes of a philanthropic nature. He donated large areas of land at Moggill to the University of Queensland, which was used for its Veterinary School Farm, as well as over 200 acres [80 hectares] of land at St Lucia, site of today's attractive St Lucia campus.

Dr James, a dedicated and generous physician was very different in character to his father and brother. However, he and his sister Mary Emilia were ostracised and it seems they did not receive sufficient thanks from the university for their generosity as Mayne money was deemed 'tainted money' by some people.

However, Dr James Mayne persisted with his aims and he and Miss Mary Emilia, in their respective wills, bequeathed Moorlands and a large fortune in money and property holdings [known as the Mayne Bequest] to the University of Queensland.

The university sold Moorlands to Legacy, and later the house and land surrounding it were bought by the Methodist Church to build the Wesley Hospital.

Following publication of Rosamond Siemon's book *The Mayne Inheritance,* Moorlands became one of Brisbane's most famous houses.

Plate 61 [above].
Photograph of Windermere in the early 1990s.

Private collection.

Plate 62 [left].
A recent photograph of Moorlands, former home of the Mayne family.

© *Pandanus Press.*

Plate 63. PANORAMA OF BRISBANE FROM BOWEN TERRACE IN 1880 by JOSEPH AUGUSTUS CLARKE. [see also plate 60].
When this magnificent oil was on display in the Museum of Brisbane it attracted great public interest.
Reproduced by courtesy of the Queensland Museum and the Premier's Department.

Photograph © Pandanus Press.

Plate 64 [above].
A recent photograph of OLD GOVERNMENT HOUSE.

© *Pandanus Press.*

Plate 65 [left].
A recent photograph of FERNBERG [NEW GOVERNMENT HOUSE].

© *Pandanus Press.*

The Governors' Residences

Old Government House

Brisbane's first Government House was designed and built by Joshua Jeays [1847–1909], who was Mayor of Brisbane at the time he undertook this work. His son is believed to have done some of the drafting. The building was erected in 1860 adjoining the City Botanic Gardens, for £12,000. Jeays undercut his rivals by quoting for sandstone from his own quarry at Goodna.

Queensland's first Government House, then one of Queensland's finest buildings, is a blend of neoclassical and colonial styles. The semicircular portico with its Ionic columns supports a roofed upper balcony with verandas and colonnades well adapted to Brisbane's climate.

The building was completed in 1862. The State's first Governor, Sir George Bowen, and his Greek-born wife, Lady Diamantina, moved there from their rented accommodation in Adelaide Street.

Between 1862 and 1910, eight successive governors of Queensland entertained official guests in Government House, but eventually the building was considered to be too small. In 1892, the Government Architect, A.B. Brady, reported:

> The house is not suited for entertainments on a large scale and is not sufficiently spacious to enable the Governor to invite or entertain the number of guests that he would wish.

The Governor also complained of the lack of a purpose-built ballroom, making it necessary to move the carpets and furniture when official functions were held.

In 1909, the Government finally conceded that Queensland needed a larger official residence. On a crisp morning in June 1910, all the furniture was moved from Old Government House to Fernberg in Bardon. From that time onwards, Old Government House was used by the adjoining University of Queensland, then Brisbane's only university.

In the early 1950s, the University of Queensland was finally resettled on land at St Lucia bought for them by Dr James Mayne. Old Government House was taken over by the Queensland Institute of Technology, later to become a university in its own right.

In September 1973, the building passed into the care of the National Trust. The exterior was renovated and the building has become part of the Gardens Campus of the Queensland University of Technology.

The Saga of Fernberg, Bardon

Governor Sir William McGregor arrived in Brisbane on 2 December 1909, by which time Old Government House was acting as headquarters for the newly established University of Queensland. He was appointed the University's new Chancellor.

Meanwhile, the Queensland Government had rented Fernberg in Bardon. Fernberg was a strange choice for a temporary Government House, considering that it was smaller than Old Government House rather than larger. The Government of Queensland was hoping to build a new and larger Government House in Victoria Park at Kelvin Grove, but had to find rented accommodation before Sir William and his second wife arrived from Newfoundland, where he had been serving as governor.

Empty houses that were inspected included Fernberg, South Merthyr, Kinellan and Wybernia at New Farm and Cumbooquepa in Brisbane. Fernberg was selected for its magnificent grounds on 46 acres of bushland. A three-year lease was signed with the option that the Queensland Government could purchase Fernberg should they decide not to build a new Government House at Kelvin Grove.

Fernberg had been designed by architect Benjamin Backhouse and was built in 1865 for Johann [John] Heussler, honorary consul for Queensland, who had been responsible for the emigration of thousands of Germans to Queensland. Heussler had become wealthy by importing European wines and farm machinery into Queensland. He married Sophia Esther Westgarth, who came from an old pioneering family. They named the house Fernberg after blending the two German words: *Fern*, meaning distant or remote, and *Berg*, meaning mountain.

Heussler's dream was to establish sugar plantations on land he owned at Pimpama. To do this, he personally guaranteed shareholders a return of 10% on their investment. Tragedy struck in 1872, when the cane became infected by rust and rotted away before it could be harvested. As a result, share prices in Heussler's Pimpama Sugar Company collapsed. To be able to pay investors, Heussler had to sell his assets. The Bank of New South Wales foreclosed on his mortgage and he went bankrupt.

The bank leased Fernberg to Sir Arthur Palmer, future Premier of Queensland, and then advertised the house for sale in *The Brisbane Courier* of 24 November 1877 as a brick and stone residence, four storeys high.

Fernberg was bought by George Judah Cohen, a merchant, and his brother Nathan. The Cohen brothers resold the house and land to John Stevenson, a Scottish-born cattle baron. Stevenson employed architect Richard Gailey to extend the house and build an Italianate tower from which it was possible to see Moreton Bay.

Gailey almost doubled the size of the old house with a new wing of 80 squares [740 m^2]. However, the conditions for domestic staff were no better. They still had to live in a rabbit warren of tiny rooms in the dark, dank basement.

John Stevenson and his wife, the former Jane Palmer, entertained lavishly, using the verandahs whose ceilings they festooned in imported Liberty silks to give an exotic effect at their parties. Like Heussler, Stevenson also over-reached himself and went bankrupt in the depression of the 1880s. By fair or foul means he managed to remain at Fernberg as a sitting tenant until his death, unlike poor Heussler, who lost his fortune *and* his home.

Governor Sir William McGregor, for whom the Queensland Government leased Fernberg, was a former medical practitioner who regarded the original earth closets, by now over 50 years old, as outdated, insanitary and a health risk.

At the time Brisbane had no sewerage and relied on 'honey carts' for sewage disposal. Sir William [whose first wife had died from dysentery] feared his children or his second wife might catch dysentery, jaundice or typhoid, all prevalent in Brisbane at that period. He wrote a detailed report to the Queensland Parliament, filled with pungent complaints about poor sanitation at Fernberg and unhealthy living conditions for the domestic staff. As the house was still lit by candles and gas lamps he also demanded the Government pay to modernise it and install electric light, then a relatively new invention.

In response to Sir William's complaints, the Queensland Government spent more than £4,000 on Fernberg. The house was repainted inside and out, new carpets and linoleum were laid, the leaks in the roof repaired and electric light and a septic tank installed.

Drought years and money problems meant the Queensland Government decided against proceeding with its costly building plans at Victoria Park. They availed themselves of the opportunity to purchase Fernberg for a bargain price of £10,000.

Sir William and Lady McGregor loved the grounds and the wonderful views across to Moreton Bay. They remained at Fernberg until Sir William retired as Governor in 1914.

In 1934, the impending visit by Prince Henry, Duke of Gloucester, and his retinue, caused Governor Sir Leslie Wilson to confront Parliament over poor living conditions for the domestic staff at Fernberg. Sir Leslie highlighted the need to extend the house and improve staff conditions or, if this was not possible, to move the Vice-Regal residence elsewhere.

The Government capitulated. Modernisation work was carried out in 1937 while Sir Leslie and Lady Wilson were on leave in London. A separate building to house the domestic staff was built in the grounds. The main house was enlarged and redecorated before the arrival of the Duke of Gloucester.

Once again Fernberg was redecorated and air-conditioning fitted for the first visit by the Queen and Prince Philip.

Today Fernberg is tastefully furnished and a selection of fine Australian paintings of the colonial era are on loan from the Queensland Art Gallery.

On open days the magnificent grounds are visited by the public. Investitures take place inside the house.

Early days at Milton and Toowong

Mount Coot-tha Road, Toowong

Before Separation, Toowong, originally known as the village of Noona, was surveyed by James Warner on behalf of the New South Wales Government. Initially, Warner surveyed the area around today's Toowong Railway Station and Glen Road [then known as Emma Street]. The land was subdivided into 40 to 50 acre blocks and sold by the New South Wales Government to potential farmers and a few property developers.

Toowong's earliest tracks and roads were initially unnamed except for Mogg-hill Road, which is supposed to have stemmed from a track used by convict timber-getters. An Anglican church was built and the tracks that eventually became Josling Street and Indooroopilly Road were hacked out of the bush by pioneers, who often lived rough in dirt-floored bark or slab huts.

The first residential development in Toowong took place in the early 1860s. In the 1870s and 1880s, large colonial-style homes and smaller weatherboard houses, similar to those in the foreground of L.J. Cranston's drawing [plate 66], were built.

Land for a Toowong Cemetery was reserved in October 1870.

Once the rail line reached Toowong in 1876, the area became appealing as a beautiful place to live to wealthy businessmen and politicians such as Sir Robert Philp, Sir Arthur Palmer and Sir Thomas McIlwraith and lawyer W.H. Miskin [after whom Miskin Street is named].

Toowong became independent from Brisbane in 1903 but lost it when the Greater Brisbane Council was created in 1925. However, the area managed to retain its 'sylvan' or wooded charm and 'rural village' atmosphere for many decades.

In the 1890s, when Cranston made this drawing, the original owners of some of the largest blocks had subdivided their land. Developments such as the Ivy Street and Lang Farm estates had begun. Ribbon developments were starting to creep along roads like Sylvan Road and Bayliss Street. These roads had market gardens owned by Chinese vegetable sellers, who carried their produce in cane baskets slung from a yoke across their shoulders. By the 1930s, Toowong boasted an excellent Chinese laundry in the centre of the village.

In the early days Toowong attracted residents who were happy to reside some distance away from the City for a chance to live a quiet life among the bush and its magnificent bird life.

The bushland to the left of the road in Cranston's drawing became the site of Brisbane City Council's Mount Coot-tha Botanic Gardens. Mount Coot-tha was initially known as One Tree Hill, after a big gum tree that stood out as a Brisbane landmark.

The rustic colonial house to the right of the road with its steeply pitched iron roof, brick chimney and verandahs is a typical Toowong home of the period.

L.J. Cranston does not appear in any census as a house owner but may have rented accommodation in Toowong during the time he sketched many of the streets in that area. His sketchbook, which is in the John Oxley Library, shows many timber cottages, often owner-built and of relatively simple construction with steeply pitched roofs but lacking overhangs or wide eaves.

Before the introduction of electric fans or air-conditioning residents tried to reduce the impact of Brisbane's fierce summer heat by planting jacarandas, poincianas, camphor laurels and native black bean trees close to their homes.

By the 1890s, houses on stumps were prevalent all over Toowong and other outlying areas. All stumps were topped with metal caps to protect wooden houses from white ant infestation. Gradually, the stumps were made longer to provide better protection against floods, snakes, bush rats and other pests. By raising floor levels valuable storage space was also created. It is interesting to observe that the Queensland tradition of building dwellings on stumps is gradually diminishing in favour of the so called 'slab on ground'.

Plate 66. TOOWONG, NEAR MOUNT COOT-THA ROAD, c. 1890 by LEFÈVRE JAMES CRANSTON. *This charming pen and ink sketch shows Toowong when it was still a rustic farming community in the bush beyond Brisbane. Wood was the cheapest building material available and its use gave rise to the unique and distinctive Queensland style of architecture, shown in such detail in Cranston's sketchbooks. This area, close to the City, is still unspoilt today and much of it is now occupied by the new Botanic Gardens.*

Reproduced by kind permission of the John Oxley Library, Brisbane.

Cook Terrace, Milton

The drawing on this page shows Cook Terrace on River Road [later Coronation Drive]. The terrace houses were built on land that had been part of John McDougall's large Milton Estate.

The first house in the row was built in 1888. A year later, the rest of the terrace was finished. The houses were part of a building project by developer Joseph Cook and the total costs were £6,000. However, two years after they were completed, Cook went sensationally bankrupt in the bank crashes of the early 1890s. During their construction the bank raised the rate of interest that Mr Cook had to pay on his borrowed finance and this probably contributed to Mr Cook's bankruptcy.

In spite of Cook's subsequent appearance in the Bankruptcy Court, the houses have been known as Cook Terrace ever since.

Plate 67.   COOK TERRACE, CORONATION DRIVE, MILTON. c. 1890, by LEFEVRE JAMES CRANSTON. The artist's pen and ink sketch shows how undeveloped the road to Toowong and the western suburbs still was at that time. Cook Terrace is still a landmark on Coronation Drive today.

From the artist's sketchbook, John Oxley Library, Brisbane.

Other speculators also suffered financial difficulties in the 1890s. Along with the bursting of the property bubble and the bank crashes there were several years of severe drought.

With their attractive stepped approaches and decorative iron lace, Cook Terrace became one of Brisbane's more prestigious rental addresses. During the Edwardian period each house was eagerly sought after by professional and residential tenants.

The occupants were glad to find residences whose rendered and painted walls and internal accommodation reminded them of the terraced homes of Melbourne or London, from where many of them had emigrated.

Cook Terrace had the advantage of a frequent omnibus service along River Road from Toowong into the city. The houses were also only a short ride on horseback or by private carriage to the city centre and there were livery stables not far away for the horses.

In spite of the riverfront location, the apartments became less attractive to tenants because of the ever-increasing traffic noise along Coronation Drive. As a result they became student dwellings. By the late 1970s, Cook Terrace had become a block of run-down units.

Subsequently, a group of doctors and dentists bought the property and reinstated it to its former elegance. The fine cedar doors, marble fireplaces and soaring decorated ceilings were restored, and sound proofing, electronic security and air-conditioning was installed. Now the houses are being let to a wide variety of tenants.

These handsome terrace houses are a landmark on Coronation Drive to hundreds of commuters who drive past them on their way to Kenmore, Chapel Hill and the other leafy western suburbs of Brisbane.

Plate 68.   MILTON HOUSE. *Photographed c. 1869.*

Reproduced courtesy John Oxley Library, Brisbane.

Plate 69.   MILTON HOUSE. *Photographed after its restoration in 1989.*

© Pandanus Press

Milton House, Milton

Milton House, allegedly designed by Benjamin Backhouse, was the first double storey house in Brisbane. It was built between the years 1853–54 for Ambrose Eldridge, Brisbane's first pharmacist. Eldridge experimented growing sugar cane on the surrounding land. Growing tired of this, he sold out to become a grazier at Rosalie Downs.

Milton House appears in the photograph [plate 68] in its golden days around 1869 when the entire estate was described as 'a gentleman's residence'. The plain Georgian colonial house had magnificent stone cellars, a cedar staircase and wide verandahs designed to provide protection during Brisbane's hot summers.

In those days the Milton area was remote from the city, a far cry from today when Milton House lies only a stone's throw from busy Park Road, centre of Brisbane's cosmopolitan café and shopping area.

Originally, Milton House had what was called the Palm Drive, from Cribb Street and along today's McDougall Street, named after John Frederick McDougall, another affluent resident of Milton House. McDougall's landholdings stretched from Milton to Moggill and included Long Pocket, Taringa, part of the cane and maize plantations along St Lucia Reach and the land on which Cook Terrace stands.

At the end of the 19th and early 20th centuries Milton House was rented out. According to J.B. Fewings, one tenant was Sir Arthur Wilcox Manning, Under-Secretary for Lands, who in 1868 was attacked with an axe by the vengeful Francis Boucher Bowerman, son of Brisbane's first artist. Invalided out of the public service on compassionate grounds, Sir Arthur retired to the peace and privacy of Milton House. Another well-known owner was the keen sportsman and medico Dr Hugh Bell. Later the wealthy Siemon family of wholesale grocers, who owned a factory on Coronation Drive and a warehouse on Roma Street, lived at Milton House. Finally, members of the Siemon family donated rather than sold the house to the Presbyterian Church, originally as a residence for deaconesses, later used by trainee teachers.

But Milton House proved costly to run and eventually it needed so much expensive restoration work that it stood empty. During the property boom of the late 1980s, the office development called Kings Row on Coronation Drive was granted planning permission by the Brisbane City Council only on the condition that Milton House would be restored. Unsightly outbuildings were demolished, but the house would never again be a private residence and the magnficent Palm Drive was not replaced. Today Milton House is used for business meetings and seminars by those with offices nearby.

The Regatta Hotel, Toowong

The Regatta Hotel at Toowong was designed by Brisbane architect Richard Gailey and built in 1887. Shortly after its completion the publican commissioned an artist to make a drawing of it for an advertisement. This pen drawing shows the delicate tracery of the Regatta's cast-iron balconies, which helped to give the hotel an air of opulence during Brisbane's ostentatious boom period.

The Regatta's proprietor, William Winterfield, dreamed that Toowong would rival Britain's Henley-on-

Plate 70. THE REGATTA HOTEL, TOOWONG.

Authors' collection

Thames in its popularity and thought that he would fill his hotel with patrons watching the regattas held frequently on the Brisbane River. Toowong, at this time, was a separate municipality from Brisbane.

The area was dominated by a handful of rambling mansions surrounded by rustic cottages. However, trains and trams failed to bring the necessary clients to fill what was regarded as Mr Winterfield's 'white elephant'. The hotel soon ran into debt.

Today, William Winterfield would be delighted to see the old *Regatta* thriving. The 'CityCat' ferry has brought increased life to the area and the hotel is always crowded with patrons.

River Road [Coronation Drive]

In the first years of settlement the road we now call Coronation Drive was a dirt track known as the Mogg-hill Road and later as Moggill Road. It ran from the outskirts of Brisbane along the river to the village of Toowong and continued on to the ferry at Moggill. The track that led from Toowong to Moggill retained the name of Moggill Road. The track was originally used by drays carrying timber to Patterson's sawmill, initially sited out at Brookfield but later moved to Toowong.

Kenmore, Pullenvale and Brookfield were part of the large dairying and timber cutting belt, which extended as far north as Ashgrove and The Gap.

In the picture below, painted in 1910, the artist conveys a glimpse of how things were when farmers in the Moggill, Pullenvale, Brookfield and Indooroopilly areas drove cattle and sheep to the market or to slaughter yards along the Toowong Reach. This road changed its name from Moggill Road to River Road around the 1890s. Just before the coronation of King George VI in 1937 the name was changed again from River Road to Coronation Drive.

Plate 71. WATERCOLOUR BY A 'SUNDAY PAINTER' NAMED WALTER BOND, *showing River Road [later Coronation Drive] in 1909. The house on the right is Robert Cribb's home Dunmore. Plate 72 shows the house in close up.*

Private collection.

The painting shows River Road in the early 20th century with yachts on the placid waters of the Toowong Reach and a large clump of bamboo fringing the Brisbane River. The residence on the far right of River Road is Dunmore House, home of Brisbane draper and property developer Robert Cribb. In 1865, Cribb sold villa sites on the bank of the river between his own residence and Moorlands, the house built for John Markwell.

Dunmore House, with a steeply tiled roof and a small turret in the centre, was named after Dr Dunmore Lang, as was Dunmore Terrace. Dunmore Lang was the instigator of British immigration to Brisbane, and thanks to Lang the remarkable Andew Petrie migrated to New South Wales in 1831.

In 1837 Andrew Petrie was appointed Superintendent of Works of the Moreton Bay Convict Settlement. He was fascinated by the area and stayed on when it was opened to free settlement. Andrew Petrie and his son John become Brisbane's first building contractors.

Another founding father was William Langler Drew, known as the 'father of Toowong'. Langler Drew was the owner of Minto, a riverside home on Toowong Reach. Toowong schoolmaster John Bowden Fewings records in his *Memoirs of Toowong* that in 1866 William Langler Drew offered five acres of land, including a timber hut and a banana plantation, for sale beside the dirt track that would become River Road. Several more fine homes were built close to River Road to enjoy the beautiful river views. The best known of all these homes would have to be Moorlands, set high above the river [plate 62].

All along the riverbank were architect-designed residences built in the affluent 1880s, whose owners could afford to employ maids, grooms, gardeners and cooks.

Further along on the St Lucia reach was the most palatial residence of all, Glen Olive [now demolished], designed by the successful Brisbane architect Richard Gailey, whose name is commemorated in St Lucia's Gailey Road on land he surveyed. Gailey bought his land from the Cribb family in 1876 and built himself a showpiece with a magnificent atrium. The house had a private gym and was surmounted by a turret with stained glass windows. There were stables, two tennis courts, a private boathouse and landing stage, orchards and gardens.

On the city side of River Road stood handsome Sidney House, owned by the entrepreneurial Thomas Finney. The house was designed by award-winning architect Francis D. Stanley and completed in 1882. Sidney House had a private jetty, a separate kitchen to reduce the fire risk and to avoid cooking smells in the house. At the bottom of the stairs visitors were greeted by a statue of Florence Nightingale, complete with poke bonnet, crinoline and lamp.

Middenbury, only a short distance away from Sidney House, has been preserved as part of the ABC complex. The house had a magnificent stained glass window with an Australian design of kookaburras and native flowers, commissioned in Ireland and shipped out to Brisbane. The window was donated by the ABC to the Queensland Art Gallery. Middenbury, set amid landscaped grounds with several weeping willows, had wide verandahs and magnificent river views. Lawns sloped down to the river and large stands of bamboo shielded Middenbury from the dust of River Road.

Plate 72. DUNMORE HOUSE, home of Robert Cribb.

Photograph reproduced courtesy John Oxley Library, Brisbane

The Brisbane Floods

The January 1887 flood was the first severe inundation in the Brisbane area since 1864. In the intervening years suburban development had spread in Bulimba, Newstead and the Fortitude Valley and scant attention was given to the risk of subsequent floods. As a result several people drowned and the Bowen Bridge was washed away.

The Week of 29 January 1887 described how,

> Nearly every house around Chester Street and the Bulimba Ferry was flooded, many of them to a great depth. Inspectors and constables were swimming and splashing about like ducks. Some of the rescued families found shelter with friends and neighbours, but many of them were so ill through the consequences of the wet condition of their homes that they were sent to the hospital.

The last statement is highly significant. In 1887 and for many years to come, Brisbane was unsewered. The unpleasant effect of the floodwater upon literally hundreds of outside privies and cesspits in the densely populated suburbs of a subtropical city can be imagined.

During the years that followed the Brisbane River flooded several times, but the most severe floods occurred in February 1893. They were the worst floods in the Brisbane area since settlement, reaching a height that remaines unsurpassed until the present day.

In fact, there were three floods in quick succession during the month of February.

All the lower-lying areas of Brisbane were submerged. The flood swept the *Elamang* and the gunboat *Paluma* into the Botanic Gardens. In Edward Street near the Courier Building the water was 2.5 metres deep. Both the Indooroopilly Railway Bridge and the Victoria Bridge were destoyed, severing the only existing road and rail connections between the city and the southern and western regions.

Plate 73. THE MISERIES OF THE JANUARY 1887 FLOOD SHOWING HOPE STREET, SOUTH BRISBANE. *This unusually fine wood engraving is attributed to JOSEPH AUGUSTUS CLARKE, who lived in Hope Street at this period.*

Authors' collection.

Numerous houses were washed down the river and a number of people drowned.

Then in June 1893 there was another inundation with water levels well above the 1887 flood, but not as destructive as the February floods.

During the first half of the 20th century minor to moderate flooding of the Brisbane River occurred, repeatedly causing damage to property and inconvenience to the citizens of Brisbane.

It was not until January 1974 that, once again, large areas of Brisbane and its surroundings were inundated by extensive flooding. This was caused by a severe cyclone followed by weeks of almost continuous rain. The Brisbane River reached its highest level since the 1893 floods.

Everything was in disarray — thousands of people had to find refuge on higher ground and trafic was seriously obstructed. Many schools and offices had to be closed, either because they were inundated or inaccessable.

Many houses, schools and public buildings were damaged or completely destroyed by strong currents or floating debris. Some eight thousand households were affected by loss of personal items and forteen people died. The damage was estimated at over two hundred million dollars.

When the floodwater eventually subsided, the smell was terrible as everything was covered with a layer of black stinking mud. Thousands of trees died and many roads were washed away. It took months before life returned to normal and years before all the scars had disappeared from the landscape.

Plate 74. THE FIRST INDOOROOPILLY RAILWAY BRIDGE, DAMAGED DURING THE 1893 FLOODS. Oil painting by JAMES LAWRANCE WATTS.

Picture reproduced by courtesy of the John Oxley Library, Brisbane.

Plate 75. MORE MISERIES DURING THE JANUARY 1974 FLOOD. LOOKING DOWN EDWARD STREET TOWARDS THE BOTANIC GARDENS.

Photograph reproduced by courtesy of the John Oxley Library, Brisbane.

The Saga of Brisbane's Bridges

Brisbane's First Wooden Bridge

For the first 20 years of free settlement Brisbane's population was totally reliant on ferries to transport passengers, livestock and goods between North Brisbane and the separate settlements of South Brisbane and Kangaroo Point. Owning the rights to run a ferry was regarded as a good business. Whenever licences to operate them were put up for tender by the Government, there were always many eager bidders.

After pressure to improve communications, the Brisbane Corporation held a competition to design the first bridge across the river to connect North and South Brisbane. The design submitted by Messrs Robinson and l'Anson was chosen as the winner and work soon began on the construction of a large iron bridge to connect Melbourne Street to Queen Street.

Sir George Bowen, the Governor of Queensland, laid the foundation stone on 22 August 1864 and no expense was spared to make this a memorable occasion.

The view below shows ships anchored in the river dressed with coloured flags, which also fluttered on shore. A podium and banners were erected, a massed military band played stirring music and the ladies of the now independent Colony of Queensland were resplendent in the latest fashions in imported crinolines and poke bonnets.

To the inhabitants of Brisbane the laying of the foundation stone heralded the dawn of a new era when communications between the separate settlements of North and South Brisbane, Kangaroo Point and other suburbs would become cheaper and less tedious. It was hoped that the old ferries, one of which was even known as *The Time Killer*, would at last be replaced by a bridge

Plate 76.
LAYING THE FOUNDATION STONE FOR THE FIRST BRIDGE BETWEEN QUEEN STREET AND SOUTH BRISBANE IN 1864.
This engraving made 4½ years after Queensland seceded from NSW still bears the title **'Queensland / New South Wales'** *while the banner between the massed flags by the river proclaims* **'Queensland, Queen of Lands'.** *North Quay and South Brisbane are still relatively undeveloped at this date. This site is near today's Victoria Bridge.*

Mitchell Library, Sydney.

and Brisbane would forge ahead in its development.

However, due to the financial crisis of the mid-1860s the Brisbane Corporation was no longer able to follow Robinson and l'Anson's original proposal for a solid iron bridge. After installing several metal supporting piers, lack of funds forced the Corporation to change the original design and, for the rest of the substructure, wooden piers were used instead of steel ones.

Long hours of work ensured that Brisbane's first bridge was completed by June 1865, less than a year after the laying of the foundation stone. The wooden bridge was intended as a temporary structure until the Corporation could afford to build a more durable metal bridge.

The engraving, shown below, is the only pictorial record of Brisbane's first bridge. The picture shows the lifting section to the left or the South Brisbane side of the bridge. The entire left span has been raised to allow a paddle steamer to pass upstream to Ipswich, where it

Plate 77. THE TEMPORARY WOODEN BRIDGE, 1865. *Unsigned wood engraving from a drawing made from the junction of Ernest and Stanley Streets, South Brisbane looking across the river to Queen's Wharf Road.*

Photograph by kind permission of the John Oxley Library, Brisbane.

Plate 78. THE COLLAPSE OF THE FIRST WOODEN BRIDGE by HENRY GRANT LLOYD. Watercolour and pencil, dated lower right, 13 June 1868. This is the only pictorial record of the first Brisbane Bridge as it collapsed slowly into the river and was eventually replaced by the first Victoria Bridge.

From a collection of drawings by Henry Grant Lloyd held in the Mitchell Library, Sydney.

would be loading wool to be brought back to the wool stores on Brisbane's Wharves.

The large open spaces shown on the picture directly behind the wharf area occurred as a result of the great Brisbane Fire, which broke out on the night of 1 December 1864 in a draper's shop on the corner of Queen and Albert Street. At that time Brisbane had no official fire service.

Collapse of the Wooden Bridge

As stated, the wooden bridge was intended as a temporary structure only until there would be enough money to build a metal bridge as originally designed. However, those involved had not foreseen that 'cobra' or marine borers would so rapidly devour the wooden piles.

One warm day in November 1867 an exceptionally high tide came up the river, exerting considerable pressure against the supports of the bridge. Seconds after a coach carrying passengers from Ipswich had left the bridge there was a loud creaking of timbers, followed by a crash. The centre of the bridge collapsed, scattering the river with a shower of debris.

The ferry owners, whose takings had dropped considerably, could scarcely conceal their delight. Their fees, which were already high in comparison to the wage of the average working man of the period, were doubled to one penny each for foot passengers, threepence each for horses or cattle, one shilling for carts or carriages with two wheels and two shillings for four-wheeled carriages. The carriage fee caused much disgust among the wealthier residents of the new suburbs of South Brisbane and East Brisbane; they had to wait six and a half years for a replacement bridge to reopen so they could drive to the city once more.

Six months after the collapse *The Brisbane Courier* of 19 May 1868 reported:

> Another portion of the bridge tumbled into the river yesterday afternoon, while the four spans on the Northside are hanging on only by their eyelids.

The watercolour [plate 78] shows the temporary Brisbane Bridge some seven months after it had collapsed. It was drawn by the roving artist Henry Grant Lloyd [1829–1904], son of a wealthy Tasmanian landowner, when visiting Brisbane on a sketching tour. He painted the four remaining spans with the Brisbane sun glinting off them as the bridge still hung grimly on.

The bridge continued in this dilapidated and dangerous state for another year, then the entire remaining structure was finally swept away in another flood.

The First Victoria Bridge

Due to the financial crisis and the resulting shortage of funds, the Brisbane Corporation was forced to build yet another wooden bridge. However, considering the bad experience with marine borers, metal piers [probably cast iron] were used instead of wooden ones.

In 1874, when opened by the Governor of Queensland, H.E. the Marquess of Normanby, the new bridge, with its elegant metal lacework parapet and footpath on each side, was the largest construction in Queensland. The Governor grandly named it the 'Victoria Bridge'.

Brisbane residents flocked in their thousands to view the opening of the new bridge [plate 79]

Since the collapse of the Brisbane Bridge seven years earlier, the Victoria Bridge provided once again the only road connection across the Brisbane River.

On 5 February 1893 a record 900 mm rainfall was recorded over Brisbane during a 24-hour period. At precisely 4 a.m. the following day an enormous wall of water, carrying entire houses and trees on its crest, was seen along the North Quay riverfront. There was a terrible crash as the entire northern end of the Victoria Bridge was swept away, once more severing the city's road connections with South and East Brisbane.

Plate 80 shows the remnants of the bridge. The view creates foreground interest with the figures of two men idling amid the ruins of the northern portion of the bridge and the wreckage of a boat which was moored to the wharf. To the right of the picture is the old prison hulk, the *Beatrice*, used as a floating convict barracks during the construction of the settlement at St Helena.

Across the river on William Street the Treasury Building, the twin gables of St. John's Pro-Cathedral and the bell-tower with its spire are shown in the picture. It also shows the building housing the Queensland Museum before its collection was eventually moved to Gregory Terrace. On the extreme right is a faint outline of the Colonial Secretary's office.

The collapse of the Victoria Bridge, the second bridge to be destroyed within 20 years, had far-reaching effects upon the development of prestigious suburbs on the southern side such as Coorparoo, Highgate Hill and Yeronga. With their road communications cut once again, prospective purchasers in those areas decided to buy instead into the newer suburbs of Ascot, Hamilton and Clayfield, which started to prosper from this time.

The destruction of the bridge also badly affected the shops and large stores of Stanley Street, and other parts of South Brisbane and East Brisbane. Several of the larger stores moved their premises back to the city or to the Fortitude Valley, never to return to South and East Brisbane.

Plate 79. THE NEW BRIDGE ACROSS THE BRISBANE RIVER opened in 1874 by the Governor of Queensland, H.E. the Marquess of Normanby, seven years after the previous wooden bridge had collapsed. The Governor named it the 'Victoria Bridge'. Wood engraving by L. Bell.

Authors' collection.

Plate 80.   LEFÉVRE J. CRANSTON. WILLIAM STREET FROM SOUTH BRISBANE showing wreckage washed ashore from the collapsed northern end of the Victoria bridge, 1893–94.

Pen and ink drawing from the artist's sketchbook, held in the collection of the John Oxley Library.

Two More Victoria Bridges

In October 1896, three and a half years after the previous Victoria Bridge had collapsed, the downstream section of a new bridge was completed. It consisted of a single traffic lane and a footpath.

The second and final stage of the new Victoria Bridge was completed the following year. It was opened on 22 June 1897 by His Excellency Lord Charles Lamington, Governor of Queensland. It was a double celebration as the event took place on Queen Victoria's Diamond Jubily.

On completion, the bridge had two traffic lanes with a footpath on each side.

This bridge remained in operation until 1969, when it was replaced by the present post-tensioned concrete bridge. The new Victoria Bridge was built alongside the old one, which was subsequently demolished. The elegant three-span bridge is a masterpiece of engineering.

At the initiative of Clem Jones, then Lord Mayor of Brisbane, one of the southern entrance arches of the old bridge was retained for posterity.

Plate 81 [above]. THE VICTORIA BRIDGE, completed in 1897. After 72 years the bridge was demolished when the new Victoria Bridge was completed.
Photograph reproduced courtesy of John Oxley Library.

Plate 82 [below]. THE NEW VICTORIA BRIDGE was opened in 1969. On its completion, the old bridge was demolished, but one of the arched entrances was retained as a historical monument at the southern end of the former bridge. © Pandanus Press.

The Indooroopilly Bridge

The Indooroopilly Bridge [originally called the Albert Railway Bridge] was completed in June 1876 after a two-year construction period. The bridge was built of steel and formed part of the railway connection between Brisbane and Ipswich. It also provided an essential link between the rapidly expanding suburbs of Chelmer and Indooroopilly. At that time Chelmer was already well established with spacious colonial and Federation houses, some with lawns sloping down to the river. As well as promoting the growth of Chelmer and Indooroopilly, the bridge opened up newer suburbs, such as Graceville, Sherwood and Corinda, for residential developments.

Unfortunately, the first Indooroopilly Railway Bridge was largely destroyed when the Brisbane River was in full flood on 5 February 1893. A wave of raging floodwater battered the substructure with trees, barges and complete houses dislodged from their stumps.

An eyewitness account stated that 'a wall of water swept away one of the 24 metre spans as though they were matchwood. The piers of the bridge on the Chelmer side gave way with a resounding crash'. By 1 p.m. the whole central part of the bridge had been swept away by the strong current. A few days after the disastrous floods the artist J. L. Watts made a painting of the damaged bridge [see plate 74 on page 95].

As a result of the destruction of the bridge, rail communications between the city and the outlying western suburbs and Ipswich were disrupted for over two years. Passengers had to be ferried across the river in barges similar to the ones shown in the picture.

Construction work on a second railway bridge had already started. But after the collapse of the old bridge that work was apparently suspended and the new bridge was built in the exact location of the old one.

Making use of the existing abutments [which may have been strengthened] would have speeded up the work. After all, early completion of the new bridge was of great importance as goods like wool, beef and hides, Queensland's main exports, could once again be railed from Ipswich to Brisbane and the residential development south of the river could continue.

The replacement bridge was designed by Henry Stanley, a resident of Indooroopilly. He was the Chief Engineer of the Southern and Western Railway. The two-span steel bridge is supported by masonry abutments and a central concrete pier. No expense was spared to ensure that the replacement bridge would be flood-proof.

The new Indooroopilly Railway Bridge was opened for traffic in August 1895, two years before the Victoria Bridge was finally restored. The bridge is still in operation today. In later years a second railway bridge and bridges for vehicular and pedestrian traffic were built alongside it to cope with increasing transport demands. A unique feature of the road-bridge, which is named the Walter Taylor Bridge after its designer, is the bridge-keeper's house, built high above the thoroughfare.

At present there are four Indooroopilly bridges alongside each other.

Seven Additional Bridges

Apart from the Victoria Bridge and the Indooroopilly Bridge seven more bridges now cross the Brisbane River.

The William Jolly Bridge [previously Grey Street Bridge] was opened in 1932 and was the first 'rainbow arch' construction ever built.

The elegant Storey Bridge, designed by the celebrated engineer J.J. Bradfield, designer of the famous Sydney Harbour Bridge, was opened in 1940.

The Centenary Bridge, Jindalee, built in the 1960s, is now part of the Western Freeway. It was badly damaged in the 1974 flood by a runaway gravel barge.

The Captain Cook Bridge [1972] is part of the Riverside Expressway and links the CBD and the north-western suburbs with the south side.

The Merivale Rail Bridge [1978] established a most needed link between the south and south eastern railway systems with those of the north side.

Downstream is the huge Gateway Bridge, Brisbane's largest bridge of all. It was completed in 1986 and is now a vital link for traffic bypassing the city centre.

The Goodwill Bridge, opened in 2002, is for pedestrians and cyclists only and links Gardens Point with South Bank.

Plate 83 [above].
THE FIRST ALBERT RAILWAY BRIDGE, c. 1892.
The picture shows that work on one of the supports for a second bridge is in progress.

Plate 84 [left].
REPLACING THE DESTROYED ALBERT RAILWAY BRIDGE, c. 1895. The southern span is placed into position by ship, while the northern span is supported by remnants of the old bridge.

Photographs reproduced by courtesy of the John Oxley Library, Brisbane.

The Brisbane River and its Wharves

The Brisbane River has always been of vital importance to the inhabitants of the Brisbane area. The river was well known to the Jagura and Ngundari people, who used it as a source of food long before Europeans arrived.

The first British ship to pass by was Captain James Cook's *Endeavour*. On 16 and 17 May 1770, he sailed northward along the coast. Twenty-nine years passed before the next British ship visited Moreton Bay, captained by the navigator Matthew Flinders, who had sailed in the sloop *Norfolk* from Sydney. Flinders entered Moreton Bay on 14 July 1799, but did not notice a large river flowing into the bay.

The next European visitors were the timber getters Pamphlett, Parsons and Finnegan, who arrived from Sydney in a small boat to obtain a load of timber and were shipwrecked on Moreton Island. They were befriended by the Aborigines and crossed to the mainland in native canoes near the present town of Cleveland. They were the first Europeans to see the river and they followed it on foot as far as Oxley Creek.

On 29 November 1823, John Oxley entered Moreton Bay on his ship the *Mermaid* and was surprised to see a European among the Aborigines on the beach at Bribie Island. This was Thomas Pamphlett, who told Oxley about the large river flowing into the bay. For the next five days Finnegan accompanied Oxley as he explored the river in a rowing boat some 80 km inland, the river [before dredging took place] being much shallower than today. Oxley's landing at a spot below today's Coronation Drive is commemorated by a brass plaque.

On his return to Sydney, Oxley reported the discovery of the river to Governor Thomas Brisbane, naming it the Brisbane River in honour of the Scottish-born Governor. Although Pamphlett, Parsons and Finnegan were the first Europeans to have seen the Brisbane River, John Oxley was given credit for discovering it, because he was the first to report his discovery.

When free settlers started to arrive in Brisbane wharves were needed to provide mooring for the rapidly increasing number of sailing ships that brought supplies and migrants to the fledgling town.

The arrival of the sailing ship *Artemisia* on 16 December 1846, bringing a load of new immigrants to Brisbane, was a signal for much of the population to flock to the Government wharf, located near the Government Store. More migrant ships followed.

From the 1850s onwards, wealthy squatters from the Darling Downs, with their wild beards and bushman's clothes, strode the wharves searching for station hands, cooks and domestics for their expanding properties, since they could no longer obtain free convict labour.

When a migrant ship arrived, Brisbane residents went to the wharf searching for servants, who were always in short supply. Unmarried men from Brisbane and the bush searched for prospective wives as migrant ships disgorged their load of new arrivals onto the wharves. Men greatly outnumbered unmarried women in the early days of settlement.

The Committee on Immigration in New South Wales was worried what *kind* of women might be arriving. In a report, written in 1845, the Committee complains:

> Street walkers can obtain a certificate to immigrate and are considered fit and proper persons to inhabit Sydney and Brisbane. Are these individuals to be the wives of reputable men of family, the household servants in our own houses, the nurses of our children and the reformers of our convict population?

By 1875, several private wharves had developed on the north side of the Brisbane River, complete with woolsheds and stores. Along Eagle Street a forest of masts and spars could be seen of sailing ships unloading crates and bales of imported goods. Steamers transported wool from Ipswich to the wool-stores on Brisbane's wharves. These were vital for the development of Brisbane as an important river port.

The American artist Frederick Schell, who painted a picture of the Brisbane River in 1887 [plate 85], described this busy area as 'a miniature Mississippi'.

In 1865 the railway system finally reached Brisbane and the river steamer service Ipswich–Brisbane–Ipswich for wool, general merchandise and passengers collapsed due to the convenience and frequency of rail transport.

In 1988, the Brisbane River became a feature of Expo; it was showered with fireworks, traversed by speed boats and skimmed by water-skiers. The Brisbane River has now become the setting for superb displays of fireworks put on by the Brisbane City Council in their River Festival, which has replaced the earlier Warana Procession along Queen Street.

Apart from a few cross-river ferries, the Brisbane River was under-utilised for public transport until 1996. In November of that year the Brisbane City Council put six high-speed catamarans, named CityCats, into service for public transport along a 20 kilometre stretch of the Brisbane River. This enjoyable and fast means of transport became so popular that by 2004 more than five million trips had been made on the CityCat.

In 2003 the first stage of RiverWalk was opened, which was designed to improve river access for pedestrians and cyclists. When fully completed RiverWalk will provide a 34 km system of riverside pathways and boardwalks.

Plate 85 BRISBANE'S WHARVES AND WAREHOUSES FROM BOWEN TERRACE by American artist FREDERICK SCHELL. *The engraving was published in the* **Picturesque Atlas of Australasia, 1888**.

Authors' collection.

Plate 86   HAMILTON REACH IN 1885, after FREDERICK B. SCHELL. Wood engraving after an original painting by this American artist, signed lower left and published in **The Picturesque Atlas of Australasia, 1888.** The picture shows the wide expanse of the Brisbane River with the road along its bank that later would become Kingsford Smith Drive.

Authors' collection

Street Scenes of the Past

Boundary Street, Spring Hill

Boundary Street is one of the oldest streets in Brisbane, dating from 1849. It was named by British migrants who arrived in Brisbane on the sailing ship *Fortitude*. The first British settlers were dismayed to find the Government of New South Wales refused to honour its verbal promise of land grants. New South Wales government officials had fallen out with the *Fortitude* settlers' sponsor, the acerbic Dr Dunmore Lang. Successive waves of British migrants camped in Fortitude Valley or rented rooms in Spring Hill. A fence was erected to keep Aborigines out of the city limits of one square mile, each night after a curfew was instituted. The track that ran along the city side of the boundary fence was later named Boundary Street.

Various reasons have been offered for the establishment of Brisbane's inner-city curfew. One reason, most frequently mentioned in records of the period, was that it was implemented to prevent theft and prostitution. There are descriptions of Aboriginal girls on offer outside pubs in return for alcohol or tobacco for their relatives, which led to street brawls where men and women were injured.

In the early days Aborigines roamed Boundary Street, the young men tall and strong stalking around like kings armed with spears and shields and their women bare-breasted. Perhaps Cranston, the artist who made the picture shown on the facing page, was shocked by their nakedness so did not include any. Unlike Thomas Baines, who found Aborigines exotic and for that reason showed them in his paintings, Cranston never depicts them in any of his works.

By the time Cranston made his pen and ink sketch of Boundary Street 'Scottish moral rectitude', combined with the Protestant work ethic favoured by Dr Lang, ensured that Boundary Street was no longer a centre of tavern brawls. It had become an area of small shops and general stores, 'kept on God-fearing principles'. Their Scottish owners were united in a desire to overcome the stigma of Brisbane's seamy past.

The large building with double-storey verandas at the left of Boundary Street was the Old Union Hotel, 'home away from home' for many Scottish migrants who relaxed there and enjoyed 'a wee drop' in memory of 'Bonnie Scotland'.

Other public houses catered for the Irish, who by the 1870s had become the largest group of migrants settling in Queensland.

By now brothels had been established around Boundary Street in a city where the male population was far greater than that of the women.

In 1923, the Old Union Hotel was demolished to make way for Centenary Park. To the left on the skyline is the distinctive silhouette of All Hallows' School, built in 1885 for an order of Irish nuns who came to Brisbane at the request of Archbishop James Quinn. It is now regarded as one of Brisbane's leading private girls' schools. Some magnificent new buildings have been added.

Wickham Street lies to the left of the picture. The street took its name from Captain John Wickham, Police Magistrate, the most important government official in Brisbane in the 1840s and early 1850s. Living out at Newstead House, Captain Wickham rode into town every day to work in the Old Commandant's Quarters in William Street and in the courtroom in the old Convict Barracks and rode back at night to Newstead. The bridle track, which he gradually wore away by riding a horse between Newstead House and the inner city, would be known in his honour as Wickham Street.

Brisbane today has *four* Wickham Streets as well as Wickham Terrace, all commemorating the same man. Between 1847 and 1859 Captain Wickham made major decisions regarding the future planning of Brisbane and acted as Magistrate before Queensland separated from New South Wales and acquired its own judicial system.

Plate 87. BOUNDARY STREET, LOOKING EAST TOWARD ANN AND WICKHAM STREETS, c. 1895. Pen and ink sketch by LEFÈVRE JAMES CRANSTON. All Hallows' Convent is seen on the skyline, just to the left of the fine colonial building of the Old Union Hotel, which was demolished in 1923 to make way for Centenary Park. Cranston gives a vivid picture of every day life in Brisbane's pre-Federation period.

From the artist's sketchbook, John Oxley Library, Brisbane.

Leichhardt Street, Spring Hill

Cranston's pen drawing shows Leichhardt Street during the late 1880s. The bulk of Spring Hill's development occurred between 1864 and 1888 when the area acquired a distinctive charm of its own. Cranston shows the picturesque weatherboard cottages of Spring Hill, clustered together in narrow streets winding up and down the hilly slopes which gave the suburb its name.

Many British settlers started life in Queensland by living in Fortitude Valley or rented rooms in the workers' cottages in Spring Hill. Some of them bought land in Spring Hill after they had established themselves and had acquired sufficient capital. Attracted by the areas flood-free location and cooling breezes they built weatherboard cottages on steep sloping land.

Due to the steepness of Spring Hill, high stumps did away with the labour of digging out foundations and

Plate 88.   LEICHHARDT STREET, SPRING HILL. Pen and ink sketch made during the late 1880s or early 1890s by LEFÈVRE JAMES CRANSTON. The artist shows Brisbane's unique domestic architecture.

From the artist's sketchbook, John Oxley Library, Brisbane.

levelling them off. For skilled artisans, or journeyman carpenters, it was relatively simple to construct their own weatherboard cottages to which many owner-builders added a riot of neo-Gothic fantasies, some more suitable to a Scottish baronial hall than a Spring Hill cottage.

Concessions to Brisbane's subtropical climate were verandahs ornamented with delicate iron lace or a lattice of wood. The verandah become popular as a space for a 'sleep out'. In later years many verandahs were built-in to provide an additional room to the family dwelling.

Major development took place in the 1870s and during the building boom of the early 1880s. Second-generation Queenslanders who loved the climate started to raise their thin-walled wooden houses off the ground on higher and higher stumps, which provided better airflow and ensured that they were above flood level. Besides, high stumps with metal caps largely protected wooden houses from termite infestation and made termite inspection easier. The spaces between the stumps were often filled in with panels of lattice, whereby useful storage space was created under the house.

Steep iron-sheeted roofs, often painted dark red [a popular colour for farm buildings in Scotland] added the final touch to what became a typical Queensland style. Some also had cast-iron balustrades and blinds that screened the verandahs.

In the 1880s Spring Hill had a very mixed population of artisans and small businesses, as well as a few brothels. One small rented house was home to Brisbane's first children's hospital, which had been founded by Mary McConnel of Bulimba House.

The charm of Spring Hill lies in this eclectic mix of architectural styles found in its meandering lanes, where many homes contain curved or high-pointed gables, complete with pointed finials or pierced and scalloped barge boards. Spring Hill, once neglected in favour of larger blocks in the western suburbs, now sees young professionals returning to inner city living, renovating handsome terrace houses and tiny weatherboard 'gingerbread' cottages.

North Quay

Allan Cunningham, discoverer of the Darling Downs, described a visit to the North Quay Burial Ground area in 1829 and noted

> coarse scrub, patches of vine-clad rain-forest and the bottle-brush trees which grew in profusion along with giant Moreton Bay figs, crows' ash, silky oak, cedar and tulipwood trees.

Some of the cedar and silky oaks Cunningham described would have been used for the interiors of the North Quay mansions, built in the later decades of the 19th century.

L.J. Cranston's sketch gives us a vivid picture of North Quay in the 1890s when it was an elegant residential area. The pen drawing shows where today's approach to the William Jolly Bridge intersects with North Quay, as well as details of everyday life, costume, transport and architecture in Brisbane during this period. The second mansion along the Quay was the original Mater Hospital. North Quay had mansions, designed by architects such as F.D. Stanley and Richard Gailey, with double-storey arched and latticed verandahs, corrugated iron roofs and brick chimneys, making them Queensland's contribution to world architecture.

Two mansions, Lesleigh and Aubigny, face onto North Quay and were built opposite the outlet of today's William Jolly Bridge. Aubigny was named by Patrick Perkins, founder of Castlemaine Perkins brewery, who was an MLA for the electorate of Aubigny. Eventually, Aubigny became the first home of the Mater Misericordiae Hospital, which was established by the Catholic Sisters of Mercy in 1906. Long waiting lists for hospital beds coupled with overcrowding on the wards after six years of its operation made the Sisters of Mercy decide to move the Mater Hospital to its present site in South Brisbane. Other owners of houses on North Quay included Brisbane's leading merchants, politicians, brewers and bankers.

Plate 89. NORTH QUAY, NEAR TODAY'S WILLIAM JOLLY BRIDGE. Pen and ink sketch made c. 1890 by LEFÈVRE JAMES CRANSTON. The artist shows fascinating details of everyday life, costume, transport and architecture in Brisbane during this period. The second imposing house along the Quay was the original Mater Hospital and these fine homes with their unique double-storey arched and latticed verandahs, steep tin roofs and brick chimneys have provided Australia's own original contribution to world architecture.

From the artist's sketchbook, John Oxley Library, Brisbane.

Rowing Clubs and Regattas

The Toowong Rowing Club started out in the small wooden shed depicted here by L.J. Cranston. The club stood on the corner of Park Road and Coronation Drive, opposite the row of terrace houses called Cook Terrace. At one stage Dr James Mayne of Moorlands was an enthusiastic supporter of the Toowong Rowing Club but as he aged he withdrew from membership. In March 1890 and again in February 1893, floods caused so much damage to the boatsheds, clubhouse and boats that the Rowing Club had to be disbanded. In 1910 a brand-new Toowong Rowing Club was founded with boat sheds nearer the Regatta Hotel.

In 1914, when Australia joined Britain in the war against Germany, volunteers were called for. Many members of the rowing club enlisted in the Australian Imperial Force and the club disbanded once again.

The club re-formed once the war was over but had to close down again during World War II. Eventually the Rowing Club was re-established in its present premises in Keith Street, St Lucia.

Lively scenes from the opening of the now-vanished Brisbane Rowing Club at the tip of Kangaroo Point were depicted in the wood engraving printed in *The Australian Sketcher* of September 1875 [plate 91]. It depicts the opening ceremony of the club and its premises. The picture shows details of cottages of the period. Later, the club moved to Walmsley Street, Kangaroo Point.

The Brisbane Rowing Club also suffered financial loss after its boats and sheds were damaged in the floods of 1890 and 1893 and was disbanded. However, rowing still continues to be a popular sport in Brisbane.

Plate 90.
The boat shed of the first Toowong Rowing Club, c. 1888. Pen and ink sketch by LEFÈVRE JAMES CRANSTON.

John Oxley Library.

Plate 91 [above].
THE BRISBANE ROWING CLUB, KANGAROO POINT *in September 1875 when opened by His Excellency William Wellington Cairns, CMG, Governor of Queensland. The engraving is taken from* **The Australian Sketcher** *magazine.*

Plate 92 [left].
Finish of the Four-Oared Gig Race at the Brisbane Regatta. The engraving, circa 1880s, shows a festive scene watched by spectators on board the Brisbane–Ipswich paddle steamer and a sailing ship.

Both engravings are from the Authors' personal collection.

A Panoramic View—1888

The artist William Clarson specialised in drawing large 'bird's-eye' panoramas. To celebrate Australia's first centenary, he was commissioned to draw the panorama of Brisbane, shown on the following two-page spread. The drawing was published in *The Illustrated Sydney News* of 30 August 1888. *Pugh's Almanac* reported,

> never have building operations been more active. Buildings are arising in all directions worthy of any town in the world. Queen Street has been greatly improved and in the same street there are vacant sites which will shortly be built on.

Suggestions have been made that Clarson made his panorama hovering above Brisbane in a hot-air balloon. This seems unlikely, although such ascents had been made by the Montgolfier brothers over a century earlier.

Clarson's panorama depicts the centre of Brisbane in great detail. Some of the buildings shown are still in existence, such as the Treasury Building, Parliament House, Government House and the Port Office. The site of the Mansions in George Street was still vacant when the picture was drawn, but construction work on that building was about to start.

The drawing also reveals the importance of the river and its wharves and warehouses. In 1888, roads between capital cities were still abysmal and ships were the most usual form of transport between Brisbane and the rest of Australia. In 1888, the Government Store was owned by the Queensland Government and housed new migrants in dormitories there free of charge. Migrants were also housed at Yungaba, then known as the Kangaroo Point Immigrant Barracks.

The foreground of Clarson's panorama features the Victoria Bridge, which would be swept away in the 1893 flood and replaced by a double-lane bridge in 1896. That bridge was replaced in 1969 by today's elegant Victoria Bridge [plates 81 and 82].

On the panorama the Treasury Building is clearly visible beside the Victoria Bridge. Set amid the trees of the Botanic Gardens is Parliament House.

Comparison between Clarson's panorama and that first panorama of the Moreton Bay Convict Settlement, drawn half a century earlier by Henry Boucher Bowerman [plate 17], demonstrates the spectacular development of the city and Kangaroo Point over a 50-year period.

Between 1885 and 1905 some four-fifth of all new migrants to Queensland were from Ireland. To obtain assisted passages, these migrants signed agreements with the Government to stay in the rapidly expanding colony of Queensland for a minimum of five years. Some of the Irish Catholics were semi-literate since their ancestors had been systematically denied access to education by the English, who colonised Ireland for centuries. Free primary schools [known as the Irish National Schools on which some Australian schools were modelled] had only been founded in 1830. Other Irish migrants came from workhouses and orphanages. By migrating to a new land they hoped to escape from lives of misery and deprivation and arrived in anticipation of a new and better future.

The Picturesque Atlas of Australia, published in three large volumes between 1887 and 1888, recorded migrants arriving by ship at the Government wharf:

> As the migrants step ashore they pass to the depot [the Government Store on William Street, the former Commissariat Store] where they stay until they find work or friends… Whole families, groups of young men and women and the inevitable lonely ones file down the gangway—some searching for a friendly face, others looking about in curiosity—the first stage in the process of merging into the New World.

Plate 93 [following two pages].
A PANORAMIC VIEW OF BRISBANE. A bird's-eye view from South Brisbane, `drawn by WILLIAM CLARSON in 1888.
*The drawing was published in **The Illustrated Sydney News** of 30 August 1888.*

South Bank — An enhanced reputation

In the early days of settlement various Aboriginal groups, including the Ngundari and Jagara groups, came to South Brisbane to fish and build their gunyahs. They feature in the painting by Thomas Baines [plate 46]. There were bora rings in an area that is now the Gabba cricket ground, Musgrave Park and Kippa-Ring.

Aboriginal groups travelled long distances to congregate at various places in and around South Brisbane.

Shortly after settlement the south bank of the Brisbane River, the spot where the Queensland Cultural Centre now stands, obtained an evil reputation as Brisbane's 'red light' area and the site of several slaughterhouses.

With its wharf, bush inns and warehouses South Brisbane was the place where bullock drovers stayed and relaxed after bringing their wagons and drays from the Darling Downs. There they could load their wool onto clipper ships and 'drink down' their earnings. Stanley Quay [later Stanley Street] was South Brisbane's first street. Attractive houses surrounded by gardens would not be built behind Stanley Street for another 30 years.

During World War II, when American soldiers converged on Brisbane, a separate area was considered necessary to house Negro soldiers; South Brisbane with its many pubs, brothels and boarding houses was chosen for that purpose and unofficially declared the city's 'black' area.

The run-down riverfront area changed dramatically when the old warehouses and wharves were demolished to create a site for World Expo in 1988.

Expo was the brainchild of Brisbane architect Jim

Plate 94.
SOUTHBANK.
An aerial view of the Expo site 1988, when construction work was still in progress.

Photograph reproduced courtesy of the Expo '88 Authority.

Maccormick, who had designed the Australian pavilions for World Expos in Montreal [Canada 1967], Osaka [Japan 1970] and Spokane [USA 1974]. Some people said it could not be done but Maccormick's idea captured the interest of the Queensland Government.

In 1986 work started on a South Brisbane site, now named South Bank. Finally Expo became a reality.

The event ran from the end of April to October 1988. Official tallies record over 15,000,000 visits, far more than originally estimated. Expo helped to change Brisbane from a sleepy provincial capital into a thriving modern city where visitors from many countries as well as locals patronise open-air cafes and restaurants. Expo made Brisbane people proud of their city.

After Expo 1988 the South Bank site was made available as a permanent recreation area. Some of the Expo buildings were retained and many additional facilities were provided, such as cafes, restaurants, public swimming pools and board walks. The whole site was imaginatively landscaped and has become a major tourist attraction for Brisbane.

The Cultural Centre, designed by Robin Gibson, is a magnificent complex. It contains the Performing Arts Centre with various auditoriums for simultaneous performances. The Lyric Theatre can seat 2000 people for operas, ballets and musicals. The Queensland Art Gallery with its water mall is strong in its collections of Asian-Pacific and Australian art, including Aboriginal works. Queensland's excellent State Library provides information on every topic imaginable.

Brisbane Convention and Exhibition Centre, built in Merivale Street, is also a vital part of South Bank.

Plate 95.
SOUTH BANK RECREATION AREA.
A recent photograph showing the free public swimming pool, which is one of the main attractions at South Bank.

© *Pandanus Press.*

Queen Street—from Quagmire to Mall

Queen Street began as a dirt track between the Convict Barracks and other structures at the Moreton Bay Settlement. In the early years of free settlement Queen Street was bordered by a straggle of huts. After heavy rain, the track became a quagmire where horses and carts bogged down in pools of mud.

The engraving below shows Queen Street in the mid-1850s. The street is bordered by a row of brick houses with tiled or shingled roofs. The house and yard in the foreground of the picture was E.J. Southerden's Drapery Store. Timber scaffolding stands in front of a house under construction. Further down the street were Patrick Mayne's butchery, a tannery and a fellmonger.

In 1853, the enterprising shopkeeper Robert Cribb installed plate glass windows in his shop, believing Brisbane was finally starting to prosper after the wool depression of the 1840s had ruined so many graziers and small businesses. Over the decades Queen Street changed and became a handsome shopping thoroughfare.

In 1887 the American artist William Fitler was commissioned to paint the junction of Queen and Edward Streets; an engraving of that painting is shown on the facing page. Fitler featured two brand-new buildings. He showed Queen Street as an elegant main street of what had become a prosperous state capital.

On the left the artist depicts the unfinished five-storey *Courier* newspaper building, designed by Richard Gailey. Brisbane's first passenger lift was installed in that building. *The Courier* purchased the latest American and German typesetting machinery.

Plate 96.   QUEEN STREET IN THE 1850S. An engraving published in The Picturesque Atlas of Australasia, 1888.

Authors' collection.

The Courier was Brisbane's most influential newspaper, owned by Arthur Lyon and James Swann. It began life as a weekly four-page journal called *The Moreton Bay Courier,* published just after separation from New South Wales. In 1861 the paper dropped the words 'Moreton Bay' as it had 'unfortunate associations with the convict past'. *The Courier* became a daily newspaper.

In April 1864, *The Courier* changed its tittle to *The Brisbane Courier*, since it was felt that most readers were Brisbane residents. *The Moreton Bay Free Press*, *The Brisbane Courier*'s chief rival, was the mouthpiece for the squatters, whose aims and opinions were often totally at variance with those of the early settlers of Brisbane.

In 1933 *The Brisbane Courier* amalgamated with *The Daily Mail*. The resulting daily was sold as *The Courier-Mail,* still Brisbane's leading newspaper, which was printed in the building on Queen Street at that time.

Immediately facing the offices of *The Courier* the first AMP Building is shown. The massive building, designed by architects Blackmann and Parks, was built in 1885 for the Australian Mutual Provident Society, which was expanding in the 1880s. This building had replaced a collection of tumbledown wooden shops known as 'Refuge Row', which had burned down several times.

Plate 97. QUEEN STREET AT THE EDWARD STREET CORNER, FACING TOWARDS PETRIE BIGHT, c. 1886 after WILLIAM C. FITLER. Wood engraving made from an original watercolour, signed by the artist lower left. The Courier Building is on the left facing the AMP. Building. Queen Street was still unpaved by 1886 but the first trams to run are shown.

From the collection of Derek and Kathryn Nicholls.

In the 1930s a new AMP Building, designed by F.R. Hall and Cook, was built on the same site. During World War II that building was used by General Douglas MacArthur as his headquarters. In his honour it was renamed MacArthur Chambers and has recently been converted into luxury apartments.

In the 1880s, Queen Street was in a very poor condition as State funds had been spent on public buildings such as Parliament House, the Treasury Building and the Supreme Court. Consequently, little money was left to pave Brisbane's dirt roads.

In dry winters, Brisbane ladies in their silk and taffeta dresses complained bitterly about the dust that stained the hems of their skirts. When it rained the unpaved surfaces were covered by puddles, soiling the ladies' hemlines and shoes with mud.

Fitler's painting shows a double-decker tram approaching from Petrie Bight. Eighteen horse-drawn trams started to run at the end of 1884 and serviced Woolloongabba, Breakfast Creek Bridge, the Exhibition Ground and New Farm and eventually went as far as the Ashgrove Terminus. In 1903, the Brisbane Tramways Company built a line to Toowong, which terminated at Miskin Street; shortly afterwards another line was opened to service Paddington. Trams ran every 10 minutes.

Tram horses would not be replaced by electricity until 1898; by 1921 some 180 electrified trams were in service. In the 1960s, the Brisbane City Council disposed of the trams and buses took over. The last tram left Queen Street in 1969. If trams had been retained, as they were in Melbourne, they would have been a marvellous tourist attraction.

Gas lighting was introduced into Brisbane as early as 1865. The globes of the newly installed gas lamps are visible on the front awning of the theatre in the foreground while shoppers crowded round the windows of Hunter's Boot Palace, famous for its footwear bargains.

In the late 20th century, Queen Street became a traffic-free shopping mall complete with cafes, open air eating facilities and entertainment.

Plate 98.
QUEEN STREET MALL NEAR THE CORNER OF ALBERT STREET.
A recent photograph shows people crowding the City Mall and the popular lunchtime restaurant 'Jimmy's', located in the middle of what used to be a busy thoroughfare.

© *Pandanus Press.*

Brisbane's Botanic Gardens

The City Botanic Gardens

L.J. Cranston, an artist born in Canada's chilly climate and resident for years in fog-bound London, came to live in Toowong in the 1890s. To Cranston, a visit to Brisbane's lush Botanic Gardens would have seemed like entering an enchanted world. The artist was fascinated by the luxuriant beauty of the Palm Garden situated near the Edward Street entrance. The mysterious Palm Garden provided a romantic meeting place for courting couples.

Cranston expressed the contrast between the lush and leafy tropical palms, bamboos and rainforest undergrowth and the primly dressed Brisbane lady of the 1880s with her picture hat, long skirt and white gloves. The introduction of the formally clothed figure of a woman into the picture highlights the unique fascination of Brisbane in the Victorian era—a subtropical city inhabited by a European population, dressing and behaving as though they were still living in the chilly northern hemisphere.

Plate 99.   THE OLD BOTANIC GARDENS, NEAR THE EDWARD STREET ENTRANCE. *A particularly fine pen and ink sketch made around 1890 by the Canadian-born artist LJ. Cranston.*

From the artist's sketchbook held in the collections of the John Oxley Library, Brisbane.

In Queen Victoria's days the Botanic Gardens were maintained by a workforce of navvies, mostly Irish migrants employed by the City Council. These men planted jacarandas and spreading palms in place of the maize plants and banana trees that the convict chain gangs had tended.

The City Botanic Gardens served a scientific as well as a social role and was considered a place where women could display the latest fashions. The engraving to the right shows elegant ladies wandering alongside the lily pond. Each Sunday afternoon a band played Strauss waltzes and music-hall songs, and a kiosk dispensed afternoon tea. A zoo full of monkeys and other imported animals amused children.

Brisbane was fortunate in that the Botanic Gardens' first director, Walter Hill, and Frederick Manson Bailey, who followed Hill as director, were enthusiastic collectors of tropical and sub-tropical plants. The combined efforts of these two remarkable men succeeded in making the Brisbane Botanic Gardens famous as a showplace of a wide variety of palms, bamboo, ficus trees and many other native and exotic plant-species.

William Traill, writing in *The Bulletin*, gives a good description of Brisbane's City Botanic Gardens:

> The visitor is confronted by a cool, dark arcade… formed by lofty bamboos. Through these stems is visible the shimmering surface of a placid lagoon, margined with floating water lilies, bamboos and other tropical plants.

After new botanic gardens were established at Mount Coot-tha the magnificent City Botanic Gardens became Brisbane's most popular city park.

Mt Coot-tha Botanic Gardens

In 1978, new and even more imposing Botanic Gardens were opened by the Brisbane City Council on the slopes of Mount Coot-tha.

Today, the new Botanic Gardens, with their wide range of climatic zones, the Japanese Garden, the Scented Garden and the Planetarium, prove very popular with overseas and interstate visitors. The new Botanic Gardens attract almost a million visitors each year. The gardens

Plate 100. THE OLD BOTANIC GARDENS [now a City Park]. From the **Picturesque Atlas of Australasia**.

Authors' collection.

have a wide range of plants from regional climates such as tropical rainforests, arid zones and wetlands. The geodesic dome, displaying tropical plants, was designed for the new gardens at the time when Jake de Vries was Brisbane's City Architect. The imposing dome measures 28 m. across and 9 m. high and contains a small pool with a variety of exotic waterlilies.

The Sir Thomas Brisbane Planetarium, designed by architect William Job, has rotating seats, allowing spectators to view a simulated sky, which is projected on a giant sphere-shaped screen. Its constantly changing programs are popular with schoolchildren and adults alike.

Plate 101 [above].
MOUNT COOT-THA BOTANIC GARDENS. Lake with totem poles in the foreground.

Photograph © Pandanus Press.

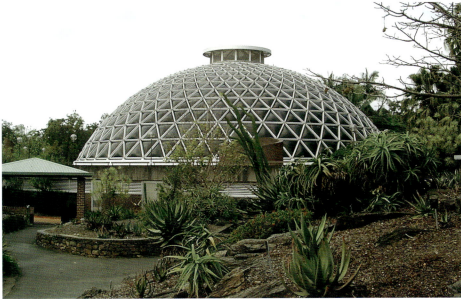

Plate 102 [left].
TROPICAL DISPLAY DOME at the Mount Coot-tha Botanic Gardens.

Photograph © Pandanus Press.

Plate 103.
A recent photograph of
SOUTH BRISBANE TOWN HALL,
designed by John Hall and Son, 1892.

© Pandanus Press.

Plate 104.   *A recent photograph of SANDGATE TOWN HALL, designed by Thomas Ramsay Hall, 1912 .*
   © *Pandanus Press.*

Plate 105. BRISBANE CITY HALL, *designed by the architects Hall and Prentice.*
The building was opened in 1930, by the Governor of Queensland, His Excellency Sir John Goodwin.
The photograph was taken in the 1980s when King George Square was still as originally designed.

Courtesy Brisbane City Council.

Town Halls—Past and Present

South Brisbane Town Hall

South Brisbane was originally a settlement of wool stores, wharves and large warehouses. In 1903, the old municipality of South Brisbane became the City of South Brisbane. Architects John Hall and Son designed a red brick Municipal Offices and a Council Chamber ornamented with sandstone and terracotta, which opened in 1892.

When the Greater City of Brisbane was created in 1925, the South Brisbane City Council was abolished and this imposing building with its central pediment, big rectangular windows and clock tower, topped by an Italian-inspired bell tower or *campanile*, lost its main role.

In World War II, the American Army used South Brisbane's Town Hall for their offices. Once the war was over the building was used by the Conservatorium of Music. Then it housed an Adult Education Centre before being bought by the Brisbane High School for Girls, Somerville House, which adjoins the building.

Sandgate Town Hall

In 1853, land sales commenced for a brand-new bay-side village to be called Sandgate. In the 1880s, Sandgate became a thriving town and it was connected by rail to Roma Street station. On weekends hordes of day-trippers arrived from Brisbane and went to the beach. In 1887, a pier was constructed and bathing huts were offered for rental, either by the day or for the whole summer season.

On 21 September 1912, the imposing L-shaped Town Hall was opened. It was designed by a young architect named Thomas Ramsay Hall [whose father, John Hall, had designed the South Brisbane Town Hall]. Thomas Ramsay Hall [1879–1950] had studied accountancy as well as architecture and became Town Clerk of Sandgate. He also designed the Brisbane City Hall and Tattersall's Club.

Sandgate's Town Hall lost its raison d'etre in 1925 when the Greater City of Brisbane was formed, but it eventually found a new role as a community hall.

Brisbane City Hall

Brisbane's first Town Hall in Queen Street gradually became too small for the developing metropolis. Two foundation stones were laid for the new City Hall; the one at the Ann Street corner of the building was dedicated in 1917 by Queensland's Governor General, Sir Hamilton Goold-Adams. On 29 July 1920, in the presence of a cheering crowd, a second foundation stone was laid on the Adelaide Street corner by HRH the Prince of Wales.

The new City Hall was designed by Brisbane architects Messrs Hall and Prentice. The building was opened on 8 April 1930, by the Governor of Queensland, His Excellency Sir John Goodwin.

The City Hall's imposing 90 metre tall clock tower is derived from Venice's famous Campanile in the Piazza San Marco. Classical Greek columns decorate the King George Square facade. The triangular pediment above the portico has a 16 metre sculpture by Brisbane sculptor Daphne Mayo. The sculpture depicts pioneers of the city.

In addition to Council offices and the Council Chamber, the building contains a central circular concert hall, covered by a copper dome. An exceptionally fine concert organ, built by Willis & Sons of London, was moved from the Old Museum at Bowen Hills to the new City Hall.

In the 1970s, the City Hall became too small to house the central administrative staff, so a new administration building was built. The Lennons Hotel, the Hotel Daniel and several other buildings were demolished to make way for the new Brisbane Administration Centre.

After the Council staff had moved out of the City Hall, its interior was restored and refurbished. Jake de Vries, who was Brisbane's City Architect at the time, was in charge of that work.

During the years that followed further alterations were carried out inside the City Hall, including the creation of the new Museum of Brisbane, which was opened in October 2003 by Lord Mayor Tim Quinn.

Acknowledgments

Susanna and Jake de Vries thank those collectors, curators and trustees of public institutions who, in 1982, gave permission to reproduce illustrations in the first edition of this book. Naturally since that date some of these paintings would have changed hands so the authors invite the new owners to contact Pandanus Press should they wish their names to appear in the picture credits of future editions.

In compiling this book, which contains some material in addition to that published in Susanna's book *Historic Brisbane and its Early Artists* [Boolarong, 1982], the authors would like to acknowledge the help of Robert Longhurst, formerly Deputy Librarian of the John Oxley Library, and of Diane Byrne, another of its librarians.

The well-known Brisbane author Rosamond Siemon kindly shared her wealth of information about *Milton House* and *Moorlands*. We would also like to thank private collectors here and in Britain, and collector-dealers including Kathryn and Derek Nicholls, of Brisbane, and Tim McCormick, of Sydney, who allowed us to reproduce paintings and engravings.

Many thanks are due to Brisbane historian Dr John Steele, author of *Brisbane Town in Convict Days* and *Conrad Martens in Queensland,* whose comments have been of great assistance. We are grateful that Dr Steele perused the first draft of this book and made valuable contributions to its contents.

The greatest possible care has been taken with proofing this complex book. Sims Editing & Proofreading Service has checked and corrected the proofs. We also thank the architect Philip Davidson for his assistance.

We are grateful for the encouragement we have received from staff and members of the Brisbane City Council.

We would also like to acknowledge how much we have been helped by Jan Hogan's excellent book *Living History of Brisbane,* by Helen Gregory's annotated edition of J.B. Fewings' *Memoirs of Toowong* and by Donald Watson and Judith McKay's comprehensive book *Queensland Architects of the 19th Century,* which contains biographical details of Brisbane's early architects. We have also cited biographical details from relevant volumes of *The Australian Dictionary of Biography.*

Local history books are more than just paper, cardboard and string. Many are the results of extensive research by authors dedicated to uncover the past. We recognise that one person's knowledge is largely built on collective information passed on by other people.

Bibliography

UNPUBLISHED SOURCES

BLAXLAND FAMILY. *Papers,* Mitchell Library, Sydney ML MSS A1322. Holograph letters of Eliza Hodgson to her sister Mrs. G. Blaxland and to L. Blaxland 1844–1852.

COMMISSIONER OF CROWN LANDS, DARLING DOWNS AREA OF N.S.W. *Letterbook. 1843*–1848.Land claims of G.K.E. Fairholme & W. Leith-Hay at Toolburra together with their Land Title Grants. Pp. 89, 281–4, Mitchell Library, Sydney ML MSS A1764121.

COUTTS, J.D.V., Early Queensland Architects, John Oxley Library, 1952.

DOWLING, Sir James. Journal and family papers 1827–1903, Mitchell Library, Sydney ML MSS A4851.

DOWLING, Sir James. Letters 1826–1844, Mitchell Library, Sydney ML MSS A4891.

FAIRHOLME, George. Letters to Leslie family, Scotland. Mitchell Library, Sydney ML MSS A 107151.

HODGSON, Arthur. Papers including *Australia. Revisited* by Sir Arthur Hodgson, Mitchell Library, Sydney ML MSS A32491.

LANG, Rev. John Dunmore. Papers, Mitchell Library, Sydney ML MSS A2211.

LESLIE FAMILY. Correspondence, 1834–60, John Oxley Library.

MACARTHUR FAMILY. Papers. Vol. 40, pp. 277–8. *George Fairholme in Paris* 1855, Mitchell Library, Sydney ML MSS A2936.

MARTENS, Conrad. Notebooks and Letterbooks, Dixson Library, Sydney DL MS 142-4.

STOBART, Henry. Journal of a Visit to New South Wales, November 1852–July 1853, Mitchell Library, Sydney ML MSS 1229.

STOBART, Henry. Letters and Journal, August 1846, October 1852–April 1856, Mitchell Library, Sydney. Microfilm FM 4/2129.

PUBLISHED SOURCES
PERIODICAL PUBLICATIONS

Art Union [later *Art journal*]. London. 1839–1912. Burke's Genealogical and Heraldic Dictionaries of the Peerage, Baronetage and Knightage. London. 1826-

Burke's Genealogical and Heraldic History of the Landed Gentry. London. 1837–.

Gentleman's Magazine. London. 1731-1907.

Journal of the Australian Historical Society [later Royal Australian Historical Society]. Sydney. 1901–

Journal of the Historical Society of Queensland [later Royal Historical Society of Queensland. 1914–

Medical Journal of Australia. Sydney. 1914-

GOVERNMENT PUBLICATIONS

New South Wales Government Gazette. Sydney 1832—

Queensland Government Gazette. Brisbane 1859—

NEWSPAPERS

[Final dates are for cessation of publication]

Australasian Sketcher with Pen and Pencil. Melbourne. 1873–89

Australian. Sydney. 1824–48.

Courier Mail, The. Brisbane. 1933–

Hobart Town Courier. Hobart. 1827–59

Hobart Town Gazette. Hobart. 1816–27.

Illustrated Sydney News. Sydney. 1853–94.

Moreton Bay Courier [later *Courier and Brisbane Courier*]. Brisbane. 1846–1933.

Moreton Bay Free Press [later *Queensland Free Press*]. Brisbane. 1850–60.

Queensland Figaro. Brisbane. 1833–1906.

Queenslander. Brisbane. 1866–1939.

Sydney Gazette and New South Wales Advertiser. Sydney. 1803–42.

Sydney Morning Herald, The. Sydney. 1831–

Times, The, London. 1785–

Truth. Sydney. 1890–1958

BOOKS

ALBERT VICTOR, Prince Of The Realm & Duke Of Clarence. *The Cruise of Her Majesty's Ship 'Bacchante' 1879–1882. Compiled from the Private Journals, Letters and Notebooks of Prince Albert Victor and Prince George of Wales, with Additions by John N. Dalton.* Macmillan, London, 1886.

BÉNÉZIT, Emmanuel. *Dictionnaire critique et documentaire des peintres, sculpteurs, dessinateurs et graveurs….* Nouv. ed. Paris: Grund, 1976.

BOSTOCK, John. *The Dawn of Australian Psychiatry. The Care of Mental Invalids from the time of the First Fleet.* Brisbane, 1951.

BURKE, Sir John Bernard. *A Genealogical and Heraldic History of the Colonial Gentry*. 2 v. Harrison, London, 1891–95.

CUMPSTON, J.S. *Shipping Arrivals and Departures, Sydney, 1788–1825*. Canberra, 1964.

DARWIN, Charles. *Charles Darwin's Diary of the Voyage of H.M.S. "Beagle"*. [ed. Nora Barlow]. Cambridge University Press, Cambridge, 1933.

DE VRIES, Susanna. *Conrad Martens in Australia and on the Beagle*. Pandanus Press, Brisbane, 1994.

DE VRIES. Susanna. *Great Australian Women*, Volume 2 [includes the full story of Mary McConnel] and *The Complete Book of Great Australian Women*, HarperCollins, Sydney 2002 and 2003.

DE VRIES, Susanna, *Historic Sydney: The Founding of Australia*. Angus and Robertson, Sydney, 1989 and Pandanus Press, Brisbane, 1999.

DORNAN, Dimity and CRYLE, Dennis. *The Petrie Family, Building Colonial Brisbane*. Brisbane, 1993.

Encyclopaedia of Australia. Grolier Society of Australia, Sydney, 1983.

EVANS, Susanna [now De Vries], with contributions from the late Professor Lawrence Evans. *Historic Brisbane and its Early Artists*. Boolarong Publications, Brisbane, 1981.

FEWINGS, J.B. [ed. Helen Gregory] *Arcadian Simplicity, Memoirs of Toowong*. Library Board of Queensland, Brisbane, 1990.

FIELDING, Mantle. *Dictionary of American Painters, Sculptors and Engravers*. With an addendum compiled by James F. Carr. New York, 1965.

FISHER, Stanley. *A Dictionary of Watercolour Painters, 1750–1900*. Foulsham, London, 1972.

FLOWER, Cedric. *Duck and Cabbage Tree. A History of Australian Costume*. Sydney, 1975.

GARRAN, A. *Picturesque Atlas of Australasia*. Sydney, 1887–88

GRAVES, Algernon. *The Royal Academy: A Complete Dictionary of Contributors and their Works from 1769–1904*.

HARDIE, Martin. *Watercolour Painting in Britain*. [Ed. Dudley Snelgrove with Jonathan Mayne and Basil Taylor]. 3 vols. Batsford, London, 1966–8.

HARPER, J. Russell. *Early Painters and Engravers in Canada*. University of Toronto Press, Toronto, 1970.

HOGAN, Janet. *Living History of Brisbane*. Boolarong Publications, Brisbane, 1982.

INGLETON, Geoffrey C. *True Patriots All*. Angus and Robertson, Sydney, 1952.

LINDSAY, Lionel. *Conrad Martens. The Man and his Art*, Angus and Robertson, Sydney, 1968.

MALLALIEU, H. *Dictionary of British Watercolour Artists to 1920*. Antique Collectors Club, 1976.

McCULLOCH, Alan. *Encyclopedia of Australian Art*. Hutchinson, Melbourne:,1968.

MAYNARD, Margaret. *Fine Art Exhibitions in Brisbane, 1884–1916*, by Margaret Maynard and Julie K. Brown. Brisbane. Fryer Memorial Library, University of Queensland, 1980.

MORRISON, W. Frederick, *The Aldine History of Queensland*. Brisbane, 1888.

SIEMON, Rosamund. *The Mayne Inheritance*. University of Queensland Press, St Lucia, Brisbane, 2002.

STEELE, J. G. *Brisbane Town in Convict Days*. University of Queensland Press, St Lucia, Brisbane, 1978.

TOOWONG, a Community's history. [eds Susan Leggett and Roslyn Grant] West Toowong Community Association, Brisbane 2003 with contributions on varied aspects of Toowong history from many authors, including Arthur Palmer, John Bray, Jenny Bigge, Margaret Deeth, Marilyn England, Helen Gregory, Carol Hetherington, Judy Magub, Bruce Sinclair and Jim McCormick.

WATSON, Donald and McKAY, Judith. *Queensland Architects of the 19th Century: a biographical dictionary*. Queensland Museum, Brisbane, 1994.

Index

Aborigines, 12, 20, 21, 33, 46, 60, 74, 105, 108, 118
Addison, George Henry, 74, 76, 130
Albert Railway Bridge, 103
Alexandra, 59
All Hallows' Convent School, 108
Appel, John George, 80
Armytage, J.C., 35, 60, 118
Ascot, 59, 80, 99
Ashgrove, 92, 122
Atkinson, Sallyanne, 6
Aubigny, 111
Australian Sketcher, The, 113
Backhouse, Benjamin, 51, 59, 80, 85, 91, 130
Backhouse, James, 17, 18
Bailey, Frederick Manson, 124
Baines, Thomas, 60, 61, 108, 118
Ballow, Dr David, 28, 45, 59
Bancroft, Dr Joseph, 51
Bardon, 5, 85
Barney, Captain [later Major], 9, 23
Barr, John, 56
Beagle, The, 31, 37, 38, 40, 53
Bell, Lieutenant, 46
Bellevue Hotel, 5, 68, 72
'Bell's Valley', 46
Binna Burra, 76
Birley, Robert, 77
Birley, Walter, 77
Blackall, Samuel, 48
Bond, Walter, 92
Botanic Gardens [City], 5, 20-23, 26, 38, 48, 65, 72, 85, 123, 124
Botanic Gardens [Mount Coot-tha], 5, 6, 87, 124
Boundary Street [Spring Hill], 5, 108
Bourke, Governor, 21
Bowen, Lady Diamantina, 77
Bowen, Sir George Ferguson, 68, 77, 85
Bowerman, Cordelia, 23
Bowerman, Francis Boucher, 91
Bowerman, Henry Boucher, 8, 10, 14, 22, 23, 26, 115
Bradfield, J.J., 115
Breakfast Creek, 65, 122
Bribie Island, 105
Brisbane City Council, 40, 58, 87, 91, 106, 124, 129, 130
Brisbane Convention and Exhibition Centre, 119
Brisbane River, 5, 8, 20, 23, 32, 33, 35, 37, 38, 40, 53, 65, 68, 92, 97, 99, 103, 105, 106, 118
Brisbane Town in Convict Days, 130
Brisbane Tramways Company, 122
Brisbane, Governor Thomas, 105
Brisbane's Wharves, 97, 105
Brookfield, 92
Building of Brisbane, The, 130
Bulimba, 4, 31, 38, 64, 65, 94, 111
Bulimba House, 4, 31, 38, 111
Bulletin, The, 124
Bush Inn, 33
Campbell, 'Tinker', 35, 77
Canning Downs, 31, 40
Castlemaine Perkins brewery, 111
Centenary Park, 108
Chapel Hill, 89
Chasely, 46
Chatsworth, 76
Chelmer, 103
Children's Hospital, Brisbane, 31
Children's Graveyard, 22
Cintra Galleries, 53
Cintra House, 4, 51, 52, 53, 65
CityCat, 92
City Hall [Brisbane], 129
Clarke, Dr Drury, 14
Clarke, John James, 70
Clarke, Joseph Augustus, 65, 77
Clarson, William, 115
Clayfield, 99
Cleveland, 68, 105
Clunie, Captain James, 10, 18
Cohen, George Judah, 86
Cohen, Nathan, 86
Coley, Captain, 8, 27
Collins, Michael, 18
Commandant's Quarters, 9, 108
Commissariat Store, 4, 9, 10, 14, 23, 26, 27, 60, 115
Conrad Martens in Queensland, 130
Convict Barracks, 4, 10, 12, 21, 23, 26, 27, 28, 48, 53, 108, 120
Convict Hospital, 22
Convict Settlement, Moreton Bay, 23, 115
Coochin Coochin, 40
Cook Terrace, 5, 89, 90, 113
Cook, Captain James, 105

Cook, Joseph, 89
Cooksland, 68
Coorparoo, 59, 99
Coronation Drive, 5, 80, 89, 91, 92, 105, 113
Cotton, Major, 10
Courier newspaper building, 120
Courier, The, 23, 121
Courier-Mail, The, 121
Cowley, James, 130
Cowlishaw, James, 65, 66
Cowper, Dr Henry, 12
Cox, Robert, 80
Cranston, Lefèvre James, 87, 108, 110, 111, 113, 123, 124
Cressbrook, 38
Cribb, Robert, 93, 120
Cunningham, Allan, 111
Customs House, 4, 40, 45
Daintree, Richard, 35, 60
Dalrymple, Ernest, 28
Daniel, Hotel, 129
Darling Downs, 8, 28, 31, 33, 35, 37- 40, 46, 53, 68, 105, 111, 118
Darling, Governor, 28
Darwin, Charles, 31, 37, 40, 53
Dickson, Lady Annie, 65
Dickson, Sir James, 65
Dunmore House, 93
Earle, Augustus, 17
East Brisbane, 99
Endeavour, 105
Evans Deakin Shipyards, 77
Exhibition Ground, 122
Fairholme, George, 8, 32, 33
Female Factory, 4, 9, 12, 14, 21, 55
Fernberg, 5, 85, 86
Fernbrook, 74
Few, A Harding, 115
Fewings, J.B., 91
Fewings, John Bowden, 93
Finnegan, 105
Fitler, William, 48, 120, 122
Fitzsimmons, Thomas, 38
Flinders, Matthew, 105
Fortitude, 46
Fortitude Valley, 4, 32, 46, 47, 94, 99, 108, 110
Frog's Hollow, 21
Fyans, Captain, 10
Gailey, Richard, 51, 66, 80, 86, 91, 93, 111, 120, 130
Gap, The, 92
Gayundah, SS, 48
Gibson, Robert, 119

Gilligan [the flogger], 21, 23
Gladfield, 40
Glen Olive, 93
Goodna, 85
Goodwin, Sir John, 129
Goomburra, 28, 40
Gorman, Lieutenant, 10
Government House [Old], 65, 85
Government Stores, 115
Grammar School [Boys], 66
Grammar School [Girls], 66
Grange, The, 76
Greater Brisbane City Council, the, 129
Gregory, Helen, 70
Gregory, Sir Augustus, 60, 74
Hall and Prentice, 129
Hall, John, 129
Hall, Thomas Ramsay, 129
Hamilton, 4, 59, 65, 80, 99
Hamilton Goold-Adams, Sir, 129
Hanson, Charles, 72
Harries, Eustace, 55
Harrison, Jennifer, 21
Henry, Prince, Duke of Gloucester, 86
Heussler, Johann [John], 85
Highgate Hill, 99
Hill, Rowland, 56
Hill, Walter, 124
Historic Brisbane and its Early Artists, 130
Hobbs, Dr, 77
Hodgson, Lady Eliza, 8, 65
Hodgson, Sir Arthur, 65
Hospital, Royal Brisbane, 50
Hunter's Boot Palace, 122
Illustrated Sydney News, The, 115
Indooroopilly, 5, 59, 74, 87, 92, 103, 104
Indooroopilly Bridge, 103
Ipswich, 26, 33, 55, 66, 68, 97, 98, 103, 105, 106
Jagura, 10, 105
Jeays, Joshua, 85
Jeffrey, George Kermode, 80
John Oxley Library, 10, 26, 87, 104, 130
John Stevenson, 86
Jones, Clem, 6, 101
Kangaroo Point, 4, 20, 23, 32-35, 38, 39, 40, 53, 65, 77, 96, 113, 115
Kenmore, 89, 92
King William's Wharf, 26
King, Philip Gidley, 30
Kippa-Ring, 118
Kratzman, Wayne, 53

Lamington, Lord Charles, 101
Lang, Rev. Dr John Dunmore, 46, 68, 77, 87, 93, 108
Langler Drew, William, 93
Leichhardt Street, 5, 110
Lennon's Hotel, 72, 129
Lesleigh, 111
Leslie, Emmeline, 40
Leslie, George, 31, 40
Leslie, Patrick, 30, 31
Lima, 46
Lloyd, Henry Grant, 8, 99
Logan, Captain Patrick, 10
Logan, Commandant Patrick, 21
Logan, Patrick, 18
Longhurst, Robert, 130
Long Pocket, 91
Lonsdale, 76
Looker, William C., 10, 22
Lumber Yard, 9, 10, 17
Lutwyche, Justice, 53
Lycett, Joseph, 23
MacArthur Chambers, 122
MacArthur, General Douglas, 122
Macleay, Alexander, 12
Manning, Sir Arthur Wilcox, 91
Mansions, The, 5, 74, 76
Markwell, John, 93
Martens, Conrad, 4, 8, 31, 37, 38, 40, 45, 60, 65
Mary Ryan Bookshop, 53, 130
Mater Misericordiae Hospital, 111
Mayne Inheritance, The, 80
Mayne, Dr James, 80, 85, 113
Mayne, Isaac, 80
Mayne, Mary Emilia, 80
Mayne, Patrick, 33, 80, 120
McConnel, David, 31, 38
McConnel, Mary, 31, 111
McCormick, James, 119
McDougall, John Frederick, 89, 91
McGregor, Sir William, 86
McKay, Judith, 53, 74, 130
McKenzie, Evan, 35
McLay, Charles, 45, 130
Mermaid, 105
Middenbury, 93
Milford, Justice Samuel Frederick, 53
Military Structures, 4, 10
Miller, Commandant Henry, 12, 20
Milton, 5, 53, 89, 91
Milton House, 91, 130

Moggill, 80, 91, 92
Mog-hill Road, 87, 92
Montpelier, 65
Moorlands, 5, 80, 93, 113, 130
Morehead, Boyd, 48, 51, 52, 65, 76
Moreton Bay, 17, 21, 86
Moreton Bay Courier, The, 37, 121
Moreton Bay Settlement, 8, 10, 14, 18, 21, 23, 26, 28, 38, 120
Mount Coot-tha, 5, 87, 124
Murphy, Dr Ellis, 80
Musgrave Park, 118
Newstead, 94
Newstead House, 4, 30, 31, 37, 46, 65, 108
Ngundari, 10, 105, 118
Nicholls, Derek, 130
Nicholls, Kathryn, 130
Nightingale, Florence, 93
Noona, 87
Normanby, H.E. the Marquess of, 99
North Brisbane, 10, 32, 33, 40, 60, 65, 77, 96
North Quay, 5, 22, 23, 26, 28, 51, 53, 55, 68, 99, 111
Observatory, 58, 59
O'Connell, Colonel Maurice, 48
Officers' Quarters, 4, 9, 10, 14, 21, 70
Official Regulations for Penal Settlements [1829], 21
Oxley Creek, 105
Oxley, John, 8, 105
Palmer, Jane, 86
Palmer, Sir Arthur, 86, 87
Pamphlett, 105
Parliament House, 4, 48, 53, 65, 68, 72, 77, 115, 122
Parliamentary Annexe, 48
Parsons, 105
Patrick, Kate, 30
Patterson, William, 76
Performing Arts Centre, The, 119
Perkins, Patrick, 111
Petrie Bight, 45, 122
Petrie, Andrew, 18, 27, 28, 31, 39, 45, 48, 51, 56, 93, 130
Petrie, John, 48, 53, 56, 65, 130
Philp, Sir Robert, 87
Picturesque Atlas of Australasia, The, 66, 115
Planetarium, The Sir Thomas Brisbane, 124
Post Office, General, 4, 14, 56
Pullenvale, 92
Queen Street, 5, 10, 12, 21, 23, 27, 28, 37, 38, 40, 48, 53, 55, 56, 59, 70, 77, 96, 106, 115, 120-122, 129
Queens Park, 21
Queensland Architects of the 19th Century, 53, 74, 76, 130
Queensland Club, 5, 53, 68, 72, 103

Queensland Cultural Centre, 118
Queenslander, The, 47
Queensland Figaro, 72, 77, 94
Queensland Museum, 130
Queensland Museum [Old], 74
Quinn, Tim, 6
Ravenscott, 39
Rayment, Robert, 51
Redcliffe, 10, 12, 20
Regatta Hotel, 5, 91, 113
Regent Bird, 23
River Festival, 106
River Road, 5, 89, 90, 92, 93
Roberts, Tom, 74
Robinson and l'Anson, 96
Roe, Reginald Heber, 66
Ross, William, 18, 21, 26
Rowing Club[s], 113
Russell, Henry Stuart, 39
Sandgate, 129
Sandgate Town Hall, 129
Schell, Frederick, 59, 105
Scott, Lord Henry Montagu-Douglas-, 8, 31, 40
Shafston House, 39
Sidney House, 93
Siemon, Rosamond, 80, 130
Simpson, Dr Stephen, 45, 55
Sleeman, Frank, 6
Soldiers' Barracks, 10, 27
Somerville House, 129
South Bank, 4, 5, 22, 74, 118, 119
South Brisbane, 4, 10, 22, 32, 33, 38, 53, 60, 61, 77, 80, 85, 96, 97, 99, 111, 118, 129
South Brisbane Town Hall, 129
Spring Hill, 5, 31, 51, 108, 110, 111
St Lucia Reach, 91, 93
St. Helena, 99
St. John's Pro-Cathedral, 99
Stanley, Francis Drummond Greville, 56, 68, 93, 130
Steele, Dr John, 21, 130
Story Bridge, 77, 115
Supreme Court [old], 4, 48, 53, 108, 122
Sutherland, James, 80
Sutherland, Ruth, 80
Sutton, J.W., 77
Sutton's Tavern, 33
Sylvan Road, 87
Taringa, 91
Tattersall's Club, 129
Tiffin, Charles, 48, 50

Time Killer, The, 96
Tobita, Tatsuzo, 80
Toolburra, 33, 40
Toorak House, 65
Toowong, 5, 8, 87, 90, 91, 92, 93, 108, 111, 113, 122, 123
Toowong Reach, 93
Traill, William, 124
Treadmill, 4, 18
Treasury Building, 5, 70, 99, 115, 122
Turner, J.M.W., 37
Victoria Bridge [first], 99
Victoria Bridge [new], 101, 115
Victoria Park, 47, 85, 86
Victoria, Queen, 23, 48, 66, 68, 101, 103, 124
Wales, H.R.H. Prince of, 129
Warner, James, 39, 87
Watling, Thomas, 23
Watson, Donald, 53, 74, 130
Weaver, John, 53
Webb, George D., 65
Westgarth, Sophia Esther, 86
White, Charles Frederick, 80
Whitmore, Professor Ray, 70
Wickham Street, 108
Wickham, Anna, 31
Wickham, Captain John Clements, 31, 53, 108
William Jolly Bridge, 111, 115
Wilson, Sir Leslie, 86
Windermere, 5, 80
Windmill [at Wickham Terrace], 4, 18, 21, 23, 27, 45, 58, 59
Winterfield, William, 92
Wolston House [see Woogaroo Asylum]
Woogaroo Asylum, 45, 55
Woolloongaba, 122
Wolston House, 55
Wright, Captain Henry, 48
Yagara [or Jagara], 118
Yeronga, 99
Yungaba Immigration Depot, 70, 115
Zahel, J.A., 72